COUNTDOWN TO ETERNITY...
The 7,000 Year Time-Line in the Book of Revelation

Shirley Ann Miller

Lampholder Publications
P.O. Box 6404
Huntsville, AL 35824
(205) 969-8996

Credits:

Unless otherwise noted, all Photographs, Maps, and Scripture quotations are from the King James Version Bible and Dictionary, Translated from the Original Tongues, 1860, as set forth in A.D. 1611.

Cover art by Jennifer M. Sayger, President, Idea Design (c)
Professional Artist/Graphic Designer
sammie@hiwaay.net or lampholder@hotmail.com

We, the Publisher and Author, declare that to the best of our knowledge all material (quoted or not) contained herein is accurate; and we shall not be held liable for the same. The Author and Publisher have exhaustively researched all of the sources and content to ensure accuracy and thoroughness, we assume no responsibility for errors, inaccuracies, or omissions. Additionally, no offense is intended against any person, group, heritage, religion, nation, or organization. This material is for reference purposes and includes ancient historical research. This book consists of the Author's original system for the interpretation of the 7,000 year time-line found in the Bible and is Copyrighted.

To schedule Author appearances write or telephone:
Lampholder Publications
P.O. Box 6404
Huntsville, AL 35824
(205) 969-8996
http://www.hsv.tis.net/~sammie/page2.html

TABLE OF CONTENTS

THE LEVITES SETTING UP THE TABERNACLE IN THE WILDERNESS.

OUTLINE VIEW OF THE TABERNACLE.

INTRODUCTION

Jesus taught the disciples a model prayer in the words, *"Our Father which art in heaven, Hallowed be thy name. Thy kingdom come, THY WILL BE DONE IN EARTH, AS IT IS IN HEAVEN..."* (Matt 6:10-11). Multitudes upon multitudes have prayed this beautiful expression without realizing the most wonderful prophecy ever given to mankind was contained in a mere 11 words.

Jesus promised His Kingdom would come, and that Kingdom would come to earth modeled after the one in heaven, *"...IN earth as it is IN heaven."* This book is about that Kingdom Jesus Christ spoke of when He uttered those words 2,000 years ago. This book is about prophecy, and about a time-line of 7,000 years allotted to mankind before the Judgment of God was prophecied to come upon all of the earth and those that dwell within it.—But God has a remnant people who will not be a part of this Judgment. They are the chosen of God, the redeemed of the earth. God knows their names—from the beginning of the Ages, a vast number of thousands upon thousands of people who's names are written in an eternal Book of Life, and of those names who cannot be found anywhere in it.

Many doctrines and theories have been written with major differences in viewpoints and opinions on the Book of Revelation, but none similarly have reflected the understanding of the heavenly kingdom in relationship to the earth.—This book contains the original documentation on this subject with a new understanding of Revelation, and never presented before in any other source. For this reason, the main theme of this work is not the evidence of pre, mid, or post rapture doctrines, nor is it a book on "predicting" the date of the rapture or the Second Coming. This book is intended to help you better understand the astronomical symbolism and imagery contained in the Book of Revelation in relationship to prophecy. Prophecy is determined in periods of Time, and out of the Ages of the Church the timing of the Seals will be revealed, out of the Seals of Revelation one discovers the Trumpets, and with the Trumpets the Vials.

This book isn't about a coming "doomsday," although some may perceive it as such, but reflects a deeper spiritual look into the symbolism contained in the Book of Revelation and a mysterious 7,000 year time-line that pinpoints a coming day of accountability. Far too many Scriptural references on the time-line render it as more than merely another interpretation.

The Apostle Peter wrote in II Peter 3:8, *"...one day is with the Lord as a thousand years, and a thousand years as one day...."* According to this Scripture, 1 day equals 1,000 years to God. If applied to the 6 days of Creation in Genesis, then 1 day of Creation equals 1,000 years of Time, and 7 days of Creation equal 7,000 years of Time. God rested on the 7th day, but what happens in the 7,000th year?

...And what about the numerous similarities and other mysterious coincidences between science and the Bible? For instance, the Greek astronomer, Eratosthenes, incorrectly came to a conclusion that the circumference of the earth was approximately 28,000 miles. Correctly, the Bible reveals the New Jerusalem coming to earth will be almost exactly the same as the true circumference of the earth-approx. 25,000 miles - (see Ezek. 48:8-20).

...And how can one explain that the first letter of the Hebrew alphabet, Aleph, meaning "thousand" and "first," can be found written in the ancient interpretation of the heavens in relationship to earth? Especially, when the "first letter for the 1,000" years of the 7,000 year time-line begins with the Aleph?

...And how can one explain how Moses' wilderness tabernacle aligns with the same descriptions for the New Jerusalem?

...And lastly, how can the comparisons between the Feast Days, ancient Jewish wedding, and the Second Coming be explained in conjunction with the Book of Revelation and the 7,000 year time-line?

My challenge to you would be read it, study it, but before you believe it, check it out for yourself. Read and study the Words of the Bible, and test the doctrines of man against the Word of God. If it be worthy, Praise God for His revelations, if it be naught, discount it as such.

May God bless you...

Shirley Ann Miller

Countdown
TO ETERNITY...

The 7,000 Year Time-Line
in the
Book of Revelation

THE TABERNACLE IN THE WILDERNESS.

CHAPTER I

"The Revelation of Jesus Christ, which God gave unto him, to shew unto His servants things which must shortly come to pass; and He sent and signified it by His angel unto His servant John; Who bare record of the Word of God, and of the testimony of Jesus Christ, and of all the things that he saw, Blessed is he that readeth, and they that hear the Words of this prophecy, and keep those things which are written therein: For the time is at hand."

"For the TIME is at hand!" The Apostle John wrote these words through the inspiration of the Holy Spirit while banished to the remote Isle of Patmos, a very small (10 by 6 1/2 mile), rocky island approximately 25 miles off the west coast of Asia Minor, and 30 miles southwest of Ephesus.   John's banishment to the island was the resulting tyranny of Domitian's reign (approx. AD. 94), who forbade the Apostle from speaking the gospel within the bounds of his imperial kingdom.

Roman rule continually pushed to suppress, even obliterate, the Christian movement in hopes of wiping out its very existence.   The Apostle John, along with his fellow Christians, were enduring horrible persecution that would continue through the first three Centuries of the gospel age.   The blood of martyrs, which during this period flowed like water was, in the language of Tertullian, *"a fruitful seed cast upon the earth, which took deep roots, grew luxuriantly, and produced abundant fruits.*" For one Christian struck down in the ranks of this ever increasing army of the Lord, a thousand new champions sprang forth; armed for the contest, and prepared to lay down their lives for Christ. *"We are but of yesterday,"* says Tertullian to the authorities of pagan Rome, *"and we have overspread your empire. Your cities, your islands, your forts, your towns, and your assemblies—your very armies, wards, companies, tribes, palaces, senate, and forum, swarm with Christians. We have left nothing but your temples to yourselves."* (1)

Although he endured imprisonment and punishment, **"...For the word of God, and for the testimony of Jesus Christ,"** the Book of Revelation is not about the life story of John, it is rather a revelation of Jesus Christ through the Ages of the Christian Church. Through the inspiration of the Holy Spirit, the Apostles' letters to the Churches, portrayed the passages in the earthly life of the Messiah from His miracles, cruel sufferings, and shameful death upon the cross, to His glorious resurrection, His promises of a future heavenly kingdom, and the final judgment of the wicked.

Domitian attempted to extinguish the testimony of the Gospel by silencing John through a cruel isolation, never once realizing the eternal light of truth would pass beyond the high, jagged cliffs of the Isle of Patmos to reach the bounds of the entire world as a banner of unfailing truth defiantly waving in the face of persecution.

For hundreds of years, the Book of Revelation has been a source of inspiration and hope to many, but also a confusing paradox of numbers, unusual symbolism, and mysterious imagery to the majority. The Book of Revelation portrays the panoramic scene of the Throne of God in picturesque images of astronomical symbolism. The most astute reader would obviously be puzzled over "locusts," "a beast with seven heads and ten horns," "trumpets," "stars," "seals," "vials," and the other myriad of terms used to describe events and time-periods. Yet, for almost 2,000 years, the Book of Revelation has traveled down through history bringing with it numerous scholarly interpretations along with various disputes of opinion. All of the varied theories have both unified believers as well as separated them, and even though people fail to comprehend it in its entirety, the Book of Revelation has the pronounced Seal of God as its authentication.

The Star Constellations and The Marking of Time

Long before astrology, early civilizations used the position of the stars in the constellations for the purpose of planting/harvesting of crops, counting time-periods from one season to the next, for guidance, navigation, and direction.

The connecting of the star constellations (not astrology) may sound strange and mostly unfamiliar to those not acquainted with time-patterns, but it is the revelation of time-periods and seasons marked by the positions of stars that the Almighty Creator originally ordained and patterned for the benefit of people on earth.   The stars represent a personally created, designed, and patterned heavenly calendar with God's own imprint as the marking of Time. This heavenly design shouts with the Creator's voice, telling people on Earth that He and He alone is Creator from both the beginning to the end. With this understanding in mind, it becomes easier to comprehend the difference between "idolatry" and "ownership."

Ownership means God patterned the stars, "meaning as the Creator of the heavens," while idolatry places (or pictures) God as the One depicted in the stars. What is the obviously, big difference? God is not the object of His Creation. He is not the One God who is subject to His creation, but His creation is subject to Him. This is where the confusion occurred between astrology/idolatry and the purpose of the heavens as markers of times/seasons and location/position. Because God created the stars to direct a course, locate a position, indicate the seasons, Feast days, and "prophecy" as evidenced in Scripture, they were not created to "guide" one's life as a replacement for the work of the Holy Spirit. Nor were they created as a form of worship or identity of the one, true God (as in the identification of God with the gospel in the stars).   This idea was mostly transferred through the writings of F. Rolleston (1862), and reinterpreted from ancient forms of idolatry to fit with Christian symbolism.

Idolatry, specifically the worship of heaven, began very early in history with the real purpose of God's calendar for the heavens reinterpreted into a corrupted reverence for the sun-god and the worship of the elements of nature.   Through time, this form of early idolatry faded into history, but its influential "seed" sprouted taking root firmly into the soil of human consciousness thereby producing the fruit which occurred in the changing of time-periods and seasons according to man's timetable and not God's.   Today, this is evidenced in the form of various pagan feast days which have been converted into Holy Days such as the observance of the Equinox (i.e., celebration of the Spring Equinox during Easter) and Solstice (i.e., attributing the birth of the Messiah to December 25th, the feast of Saturnalia and birthday of Tammuz).

In separating some of the myths from the legends, the true, Godly purpose of time-periods (and prophecy) can be calculated from the ancient star patterns found in the constellations.   It then becomes clear how a remnant of the true calendar still survives today; and it is this process of viewing the true calendar through the constellations that produces the time-line of Abraham, and the time-line of Abraham reflects the time-periods utilized to count the "Ages" of Man.   In the Bible, these time-periods are calculated in approximately four different ways: the time from Creation to the End of Time, from the First Adam to the Second Adam, the Messiah (Jesus Christ), from the time of the establishment of the Covenant with Abram (Abraham) to the Birth of the Messiah, and from the birth of the Messiah (the beginning of the Church Ages) to the End of Time.

This time-period can be measured and counted.   They are periods of time, known as Ages, rounded into whole numbers and broken down into approximate lengths, as follows:

THE GREAT AGE
First Age:
Creation to Deluge
Babel to Abraham
4,000-2000 B.C.E. = 2,000 years
In comparison to Genesis' Creation: The 1st and 2nd Day

Second Age:
Abraham to Messiah
2,000 B.C.E.-A.D. 0 = 2,000 years
In comparison to Genesis' Creation: The 3rd and 4th Day

Third Age:
Messiah 1st Coming
A.D. 1 - the year 2,000 = 2,000 years
In comparison to Genesis' Creation: The 5th and 6th Day

Fourth Age
Messiah 2nd Coming
Sometime around or soon thereafter
A.D. 2,000/2,001
In comparison to Genesis' Creation: The 7th Day

This breakdown of the Ages reveals the 6 Ages of Man ending with the 3rd Age around the year A.D. 2,000/2,001, and the 4th Age begins with the equivalent of the beginning of the 7,000th Year occurring after A.D. 2,001. In the following chapters, it will become very clear how the ancient prophets aligned prophecy with this calculation of time-periods. The prophecies were based on an Age of 2,000 years divided in half resulting in 1,000 year divisions of time-periods. So an AGE equals approximately 2,000 years, but THE MILLENNIUM equals one-half of an Age or 1,000 years.

God gave Earth a key to the calculation of time-periods in Genesis 1:14, *"Let there be lights in the firmament of the heaven to divide the day* [sun] *from the night* [moon]*; and let them be for signs* [the constellations] *and for seasons* [the Equinox and Solstice points], *and for days* [the marking of Time], *and years* [the Precession of the Equinox]*...he made the stars* [for determining Time] *also...."* This process comes by way of understanding the movements of the heavens as God's calendar, and a perfect example of this can be found in the comparison between the Wilderness Tabernacle of Moses (The Holy Place and Holiest of Holies), the counting of time-periods, and the End of the Ages found in the Book of Revelation.

An Earthly Sanctuary and A Heavenly Sanctuary

One fact that the majority of Christians agree upon is that the Book of Revelation portrays prophecy through the time-periods of history (even though history may be separated into thousands of years); yet, because it reveals prophecy doesn't mean that it is a book of mysticism. One can and should understand prophecy based upon the plain and clear meanings contained in the entire harmony of Scripture. This can be seen in the way the Book of Revelation parallels many passages in both the Old and New Testaments.

For instance, John's gospel reveals the work of the Messiah in His heavenly kingdom, *"In my Father's house are many mansions...I go to prepare a place for you. And if I go and prepare a place for you, I will come again, and receive you unto myself; that where I am, there ye may be also"*(John 14:1-3).—Within this passage of John 14, lies the important key that will lead to a deeper understanding of the Book of Revelation.

The "key" here is in the understanding of what Jesus means by a "heavenly Kingdom" and this Kingdom is best understood as it parallels that of Moses' Wilderness, "earthly sanctuary." The heavenly Kingdom (the New Jerusalem) reveals the abode, or realm, of the Most High God in His Throne Room just as the Wilderness Sanctuary reveals the "earthly abode" of the Most High God (Exodus 25:8, 9; Acts 7:44; Hebrews 3:1-6; 9:1, 21-24).

Both the earthly Sanctuary and the heavenly Sanctuary are symbolized in words that describe the sun, moon, and stars; therefore, it would be very difficult to define the symbolism without an elementary understanding of the Hebrew heavens. This combination of the heavens and the Bible makes many Christians rather nervous for fear of entering into the occult; yet, somehow most forget that God created the heavens for a purpose—the intent here is to further understand God's real purpose. The great astronomer and mathematician, Rabbi Avraham Ibn Ezra (1089-1164) explained this well when he once wrote, *"...the heavens provide man with clues as to the working of the universe"* and *"whoever knows the way of the spheres has knowledge of the divine."* The two sanctuaries depict the realm of God, but interestingly, both the "earthly" and "heavenly" sanctuaries contain the elements and measurements of time-periods.

For example, in a prayer to the Everlasting God, Moses' surrenders, *"For a thousand years* [1,000 years] *in thy sight are but as yesterday* [one day] *when it is past, and as a watch in the night...So teach us to number our days, that we may apply our hearts unto wisdom"* (Psalm 90:4, 12).

At first glance, it would be easy to describe this passage as merely a symbolic expression meaning that God surpasses beyond our calculation of time, and of course, this statement would be true. To Him, time has no bounds or specific lengths, but to mankind time is an element of nature that is reflected in our very existence beginning from the moment of birth to the last breath. When we compare this prayer of Moses to the entirety of Scripture, it becomes evident that Moses intended to convey another meaning. Psalm 90 marks a specific period of time as in 1 day = 1,000 years.

According to the Bible, God, the Creator, is the One Who declares *"the end from the beginning, and from ancient times the things that are not yet done..."* (Isaiah 46:10). The symbolism of time-periods are patterns formed according to the movements of the heavens, and it is God who *"...changeth the times and the seasons...and...giveth wisdom unto the wise, and knowledge to them that know understanding"* (Dan. 2:21).

This example of 1 day = 1,000 years is also found written in the Book of Revelation, Chapter 20, and this comparison has a far greater significance when looking at the number in its symbolic expression in comparison to prophecy.

In Genesis, the Bible reveals that God created the world in 6 Days, and on the 7th Day He rested. Therefore, the number 7, in mankind's understanding of God's timetable, refers to a time of "completeness." In Revelation 20, John writes of this concept in terms of 1,000 years through the eyes of the Millennium—(Millennium means 1,000 years). If you multiply 6 Days x 1,000, the number equals 6,000, and the 7,000th year was a year of "rest." Just as in the Days of Creation when God rested on the 7th Day, the 7,000th year (the Millennium) is an "eternal" day of rest for man. The 7,000th year represents mankind's completion according to God's time plan for Earth.

Revelation 20 depicts the 1,000 years of the Millennium divided into 6 periods of time (6 x 1,000 = 6,000 years).

(1) Satan bound for 1,000 years (vs. 2);
(2) Satan would not deceived the nations until the end of the 1,000 years (vs. 3);
(3) The Saints of God lived and reigned with Christ for 1,000 years (vs. 4);
(4) The rest of the dead lived not again until the 1,000 years were finished (vs.4);
(5) This is the first resurrection of those who will be priests and reign with God for 1,000 years (vs. 6);

(6) After the 1,000 years were expired, Satan is loosed to deceive the nations (vs. 7).

NOTE: This comparison will be covered in-depth in later chapters on the 6 Ages of man (6 Ages x 1,000 years = 6,000 years) from the time of Adam to Abraham to the End of the Ages.

Another example of the time-periods counting to the Millennial Rest of the 7,000th Day is reflected in the parables, and the Messiah explained this in Mark 4:11, *"Unto you it is given to know the mystery of the kingdom of God: but unto them that are without, all these things are done in parables."* It would later become evident to Jesus' followers that the parables could be clearly understood, but only through an enlightened mind and the spiritual insight given by the power of the Holy Spirit. But this passage of Scripture also reveals those who reside in the Kingdom of God during the 7,000th Day (believers) and those who are left on the outside (unbelievers). This confused the Pharisees when they came to Jesus *"seeking of him a sign from heaven"* (Mark 8:11).—But what were they really asking?

There is a deeper spiritual significance to Mark 8 than what appears on the surface. The Pharisees really wanted Jesus to give them "a sign" or some kind of evidence in the "signs" (the timing) of heaven. They knew Jesus feeding the "4,000" revealed a time-period from Adam to their present day, but the Pharisees refused to believe that Jesus Christ was the fulfillment of the promise (the "last Adam"). That's why Jesus said, *"Why doth this generation seek after a sign"* (vs. 12)? Then Jesus turned to the disciples and revealed the true meaning.

In the prophetic, as well as spiritual, significance, Jesus spoke of the 7,000th year when He asked, *"And when the seven* [7,000th year] *among four thousand* [4,000th year has passed], *how many baskets full of fragments* [the remnant] *took ye up* [redeemed from the earth]*? And they said, Seven"* (vs. 20). This is a prophetic picture of the Millennial reign of the 7th Day rest (7,000th year) and the FEAST OF TABERNACLES (Ex.

31:13). The 7,000th year is the celebration of the Messianic kingdom, *"...Behold, the TABERNACLE of God is with men, and he will DWELL with them..."* (Rev. 21:3). That is why Jesus asked the disciples, *"How is that ye do not understand?"* (vs. 21).

These examples of time-periods marked by the stars in the constellations, the 1,000-7,000th year Ages, and the comparison between Psalm 90:4 and Revelation 20 are clearly evident in the "earthly" wilderness Sanctuary:

Inside the earthly sanctuary, Moses placed four, equally-made pillars, and inside the pillars was found a room called The Holy of Holies—the remaining area of the room contained the Tabernacle, The Holy Place. The Tabernacle was patterned after the system of the world, but The Most Holy Place was the realm of the Most High God fashioned as the New Jerusalem with the Third Temple descending from heaven (Torah, Rashi).

Only the *"wise hearted"* women and *"wise men"* of the Children of Israel, *"wrought all the work of the sanctuary"* (Ex. 35-36).   These were the workers filled with wisdom and understanding of the Holy Days of the Lord and also the astronomy of the heavens—because the earthly Sanctuary was patterned after the heavenly one.

This becomes obvious when studying the forms of construction in the Wilderness Sanctuary as they align with Feast days (this will be covered later). When patterning the earthly Sanctuary after the heavenly one, a good comparison can be found in the various materials used for construction, and one example in particular can be found in the linen curtains for the Tabernacle.

The linen curtains were made with 50 loops (Ex. 36:12). In the 48 boards (10 cubits high by 1.5 cubits wide) made with shittim wood overlaid with gold (Ex. 36:20-34) was found the earthly representation of a day equals 1,000 years. The Tabernacle boards stood upward reaching toward heaven -

20 boards for the South, 20 boards for the North, 6 boards for the West with 2 corner boards for the sides, and the entrance to Tabernacle faced EAST. The 1,000 years can be broken down into days, months, and years as follows:

♦   24 hours = 1 day; 48 hours = 2 days; 2 days = 2,000 years; 48 boards times 1.5 cubits = 72 hours or 3 days). Two thousand years divided by 3 Ages of mankind = 666, and 3 Ages multiplied times 2,000 years equals 6,000 years. As stated earlier, the 3 Ages begin with the time-period from Adam to the Covenant of Abraham and end with the 3rd Age. This calculation of the Ages was marked by the placement of the constellations among the stars of heaven. If you will observe the heavens as the canopy or "tabernacle" of the Earth, this scenario becomes even clearer. The stars mark the passage of time just like a clock marks the time of day. It has been approximately 2,000 years since the finished work of Jesus Christ, and the Adamic time-line nears the end of the 6,000th year.

Why begin with the Adam and the Covenant of Abraham? The Bible reveals a number of Covenants God made with His people, but there are 2 specific Covenants indicated by the 6,000 year time-line. One is the Covenant God made with "man" (all people, men and women) in general and the Second is the Covenant promise God made with Abraham.

In Genesis 12:1-3 and 17-:1-9, the Bible tells us of a special Covenant, or promise, between the man named Abraham, "father of the faithful" and God. *"Now the Eternal had said unto Abram, Get thee out of thy country, and from thy kindred, and from thy father's house, unto a land that I will show thee: And I will make of thee a great nation, and I will bless thee, and make thy name great; and thou shalt be a blessing: And I will bless them that bless thee, and curse him that curseth thee: and in thee shall all families of the earth be blessed...And I will establish my covenant between me and thee and thy seed* [plural, like the millions of countless stars in heaven] *after thee in their generations for an everlasting covenant, to be a God unto thee, and to thy seed after thee.*"

These two Covenants are depicted in God's interaction with man from the 1st Adam to the 2nd Adam, Jesus Christ, totalling 6,000 years. This time-period including the entire 7,000 year time-line can also be found in understanding the deeper spiritual significances of the Wilderness Sanctuary.

The Holy Place

(1) Located on the North side of the temple was the table of 12 unleavened loaves of bread (showbread) made from 24 tenths of unleavened flour divided into two stacks of six each.

♦ 24 tenths of unleavened flour for the showbread of which only two heaps were baked on the (6th) day before the Sabbath (7th) Day making 12 loaves divided by 2 and placed in stacks of 6 loaves each. The showbread is also representative of time broken down into hours, days, and years:

> 24 hrs = 1 day
> 72 hrs = 3 days
> 72 hrs x 2 (72 hrs of 3 days) = 144
> 144 divided by 24 hrs = 6 days
> 12 months x 12 Tribes = 144
> 24,000 (approx.) male Levites served as
>   Priests x 6 days = 144,000
> 24,000 male Levites from each of 12 Tribes
>   divided = 2,000 years
> 2,000 years = 1 Age
> Ages from the Abrahamic Covenant = 3 Ages
>   x 2,000 yrs = 6,000 years

Every "seven" days, in accordance with the Seventh Day Sabbath, the old loaves were replaced with new ones. According to Josephus, these 12 loaves denoted the 12 months of the year, but it would appear the loaves had a far greater significance. The stacked loaves of six brought to remembrance the Northern Hemisphere and the other stack of six, the Southern Hemisphere along with the 12 tribes of Israel, *"...and the stones were according to the names of the children of Israel, twelve..."* (Exodus 39:14). In other words, the picture of the sphere of heaven and Earth was a symbol of the inheritance of the 12 tribes of the Children of Israel—a picture of both the heavenly abode of God and the earthly tabernacle. This will become even more evident in later chapters of the Book of Revelation in reference to the Trumpets, the "oil and the wine" (Rev. 6:6) and the Sealed 144,000 of the Tribes of Israel (Rev. 7) (144,000 Sealed divided by 24 Elders = 6,000 years; 12 months = 1 yr x 12 Tribes = 144).

(2) The entrance to the tabernacle faced the East with the rising sun—located near the Southern wall against the table, and facing South and East, was the seven branched, golden candlestick made with 70 ornaments. The golden candlestick with seven lamps, as Josephus explains represented the "seven" planets (including the sun and moon) and their course. (2) NOTE: Revelation 1:12 & 1:20 reveal the same astronomical symbolism in a depiction of the candlesticks and the Seven Churches.

The seven lamps were only lighted in the evening (Lev 24:3), except for the central lamp during the day, just as the darkness of the heavens at night hang the planets suspended in space. The 70 ornaments were the branches of the candlestick divided into 70 parts that typified the Decani, or 70 divisions of the planets.

(3) Located between the candlestick and the table just before the Veil was the golden-plated, Altar of Incense (Ex. 30:2, 7, 8; Rev. 3-8).

♦ **"A cubit shall be the length thereof, and a cubit the breadth thereof; foursquare shall it be: and two cubits shall be the height..."** (Ex. 30:2)

Here 1 cubit = 1,000 years; the shape has 4 sides

square = 4,000 years; the height is 2 cubits = 2,000 years, and the total sum is 6,000 years.

♦   The four vials represented the four elements of matter:

> the fine linen of flax: Earth
> the purple of the sea: Water
> the blue: Air
> the scarlet: Fire

Philo, a Greek philosopher (approx. B.C.E. 20-A.D.50), gives a similar description of the mystical aspects of the tabernacle, but keep in mind, Philo's perspective came from mostly from his views on Greek cosmology and not Hebrew. With the passing of the Age of the First Century Jewish-Christian, much of the early understanding of the time-line of the Ages has been reinterpreted into occultic and pseudo-scientific philosophies like astrology, and this can be viewed in the way Philo's interpretation was later incorporated into the Roman Church, but forbade by God in the Wilderness (Lev. 19:26).

Philo determined the vestments of the High Priest were made of linen (Earth), the blue denoted the sky or Air, and the Ephod revealed that God made the universe with four elements. The Breastplate was situated in the center of the Ephod, here representing the Earth as the center of the world.—Actually Philo's interpretation was incorrect, because the Breastplate represented a symbolic future look at the New Jerusalem (The Throne of God) in the midst of the world.

The girdle worn round about the High Priest signified the ocean that surrounds the outer atmosphere of the universe. The sardonyxe stones on the High Priest's shoulders were emblems of the sun and moon, and the 12 stones were the months of the year. (3) Here is a perfect example of the Sun-Clad Woman of Revelation 12 and the New Jerusalem of Revelation 20.

Keep in mind that before the Fall of Man, the Earth was perfectly designed as the Kingdom of Heaven, or the Abode of

God, His Throne. Therefore, John, in the Book of Revelation, is viewing the Earth through its process of transformation, restoration, and the eventual establishment of the New Earth—New Jerusalem again as the Abode of God.

The first believers in the Messiah were all Jewish, or Messianic Christians, who were redeemed by the Blood of the Savior, continuing in the faith of Christianity, but remained in the practice of the Judaistic festivals. After the deaths of all of the first Apostles, Messianic Judaism became emersed into Gentile Christianity until finally becoming absorbed and replaced by the Church.

The Holy of Holies

Within the Veil of the tabernacle was found the most holy place (or The Holy of Holies), where the Sacred Ark of the Covenant held the Ten Commandments (Hebrew 9:1-5; Rev. 11:19), a special symbol of God's presence surmounted by the Cherubim with faces bent down and their wings meeting in the center.

If all of these comparisons sound strange, remember, scripture confirms the association of the earthly Sanctuary with the heavenly one. According to Hebrew's 9:21-28, *"...the tabernacle, and all the vessels of the ministry..."* were *"...patterns of things in the heavens."* The heavens depicted the Tabernacle of Moses, the 12 tribes of Israel, the 12 tribes possession of the Promised Land, and the configurations of the New Jerusalem of Revelation.

Earthly sacrifices were purified with blood of animals, among them sheep, he-goats, and bulls, and *"...It was therefore necessary that the patterns of things in the heavens should be purified with these; but the heavenly things themselves with better sacrifices than these."* Unlike the earthly sanctuary whereby the priests made atonement once every year (Hebrews 9:7), Jesus Christ, the better sacrifice, made an atonement with His Blood, *"once and for all,"* *"...but now once in the end of the world hath he appeared to put away sin by the sacrifice of himself."*

And so John, in speaking of Jesus Christ wrote, *"The Word became flesh and dwelt [tabernacled] among us" (John 1:14).* This same expression carries over into the Book of Revelation where the ancient Tabernacle, as the dwelling of God, found its antitype in the divine, human nature of Jesus Christ, *"The Tabernacle of God is with men."*

The Tabernacle, Feast Days, and The Seven Churches

Much of the Book of Revelation was symbolized in imagery taken from the earthly tabernacle of Moses and interpreted into the language of the Jewish Festivals. This comparison can be found in the ancient Feast Days.

The Book of Revelation mentions Seven Churches, and throughout this book keep in mind, as reference, the aforementioned examples with the following numbers from the earthly tabernacle and seven Feasts of Israel:

(1)   12 tribes; 12 months of the year;

3 tribes on each of the 4 sides of the Tabernacle

Entrance to Tabernacle faced EAST,

but Tabernacle had 4 sides NORTH,

SOUTH, EAST, and WEST as the

4 corners of the Earth; UP and DOWN

as the foundations and the heavens;

24,000 approx. (23,880) male Levite priests

divided by 2,000 = 12 rounded to the

highest number)

6 tribes went before the Tabernacle and

6 tribes after

12 eminent spies sent to Canaan - 1 from each

tribe - who spent 40 days scouting the land

(2)   7th day Sabbath; 7 High Sabbaths during one

year; God rested on the 7th Day (Gen:2)

Rest from working every 7th day - Sabbath

Rest from planting every 7th yr - Sabbatical year

7 x 7 years = 49; 50th year is the Year of Jubilee
(meaning Liberty) beginning on the Day of
Atonement the Trumpet will sound (Lev. 25)

120 yrs (Gen. 6:3) x 50th yr of Jubilee=6,000 yrs

Every 7th month had 3 feasts; the number 7
appears approx. 287 times in the O. T.
and the word seventy is used 56 times

(3)   7 branched, golden candlestick made with

70 ornaments (weeks of days)
(representative of Sukkot and
Feast of Lights (Zechariah 14:16-19)

70 weeks x 7 days = 490 days
(side note: 70 yr. captivity (Jer. 25:11;
desolations (Dan. 9:2, 24); Rome destroyed
Temple in A.D. 70; Pesach which is Passover;
1948 Israel became nation after 2,000 yr
dispersion)

(4)   24 tenths of unleavened flour for the
showbread of which only two heaps were
baked on the (6th) day before the Sabbath
(7th) Day making

12 loaves divided by 2 and placed in stacks of
6 loaves each

24 hrs = 1 day

72 hrs = 3 days

72 hrs x 2 (72 hrs of 3 days) = 144

144 divided by 24 hrs = 6 days

It is very important to remember that the Feast days are
not exclusively Jewish feasts, but historically traditional and
prophetically future Feast days of the Lord. They reveal both

the First and Second Coming of Jesus Christ, as evidenced in the Hebrew word for feast meaning, "rehearsal for a set event, and the word for "season" ['mow`ed, mo-ade'] meaning: an "appointed place, meeting or time, a sacred season, or set feast. And the only way to mark the "time periods" or "seasons" of feasts was through the observation of the "sun" and "moon." This was the only calendar available to early civilizations. It is a form of astronomy, not astrology, and observed through the Jewish feasts, the Jewish wedding (to be covered later), and the time-line of the Church Ages.

The following seven feasts and seven seasons reveal the interconnection between both the Old Testament and the New Testament, between the feast days and the days of fulfillment:

SEVEN FEASTS AND SEVEN SEASONS
SPRING FESTIVALS
(FORMER RAIN - Hosea 6:3; Joel 2:23, James 5:7-8)
THE MESSIAH'S FIRST COMING

(1)   In the month of Nisan (or Aviv, Abib-March/ April), the beginning of the Jewish year, on the 14th day of the lunar month at twilight-according to Josephus when the sun was in the constellation of Aries (astronomy not astrology). (Ex. 12:2); *"the sun passed the equinox and was in Aries* (en krio tou heliou kathestotos)." (4) This was the month the children of Israel were delivered from their bondage in Egypt, and when they observed the celebration of the **PASSOVER** (Pesach) of the Lord.

God instructed Israel to slay the Paschal "lamb" and the calendar of the heavens was then associated with the stars of the constellation of Aries—when the Vernal Equinox moved out of the constellation of Taurus into Aries; and this was established by the Jewish Passover, or Pasach. Thereafter, until the abolishment of the sacrifice, the 10th day of the first month of any given year, was the sacrifice of the Passover lamb: *"...And this day shall be unto you for a memorial; and ye shall keep it a feast to the Lord throughout your generations..."* (Exodus 12:14; Leviticus 23:4-8).

♦ Jesus Christ, the Passover Lamb of God, without wrinkle, spot, or blemish, sacrificed for the sins of the world: *"...When I see the blood, I will pass over you, and the plague shall not be upon you to destroy you..."* (Exodus 12:13; Isaiah 53:7; John 1:29; I Corinthians 5:7). The shed blood on the door posts of the Israelites' homes portrays the symbol of Jesus Christ's shed blood as an atonement for sin, and just as the Death Angel passed over the Israelites, the penalty of eternal death passes over those who call upon the name of Jesus Christ for forgiveness of sin (Isaiah 53:7; Romans 6:23; John 1:29).

(2)   The Feast of **UNLEAVENED BREAD** (Hag Ha Matzah) succeeds the Passover on the 15th day of the month for "7" days of eating unleavened bread; the meal of lamb and departure from Egypt; a reminder of God's protection during the plagues in Egypt (Leviticus 23:4; Ex. 23:5); leaven is a type of "sin;" a discarding of the old leaven because Jesus Christ our Passover Lamb also has been sacrificed (1 Cor. 5:7-8).

♦ Jesus Christ (the Bread of Life—sinless, pure), broken at The Feast of Unleavened Bread. Leavening (the yeast), when mixed with dough and baked, causes bread cakes to rise. Leavening is a type of sin (see Matthew 16:5-12). *"I am the living bread which came down from heaven: if any man eat of this bread, he shall live for ever: and the bread that I will give is my flesh, which I will give for the life of the world"* (John 6:48-51).

(3)   The Feast of **FIRST FRUITS** (Yom HaBikkurim) occurs on the 16th day of the month; Feast of Barley; the day after the Weekly Sabbath (the first Sunday after the 15th of Nisan (Aviv). Traditionally, the Feast of First Fruits celebrated the giving of the Torah at Mount Sinai. Harvest Offering First day after the Sabbath after Passover (Sunday) Leviticus 23:7-9: *"Speak unto the children of Israel, and say unto them, `When ye be come into the land which I give unto*

you, and shall reap the harvest thereof, then ye shall bring a sheaf of the firstfruits of your harvest unto the priest. And he shall wave the sheaf before the Lord, to be accepted for you...." This is the festival of the Resurrection of the Messiah, Jesus Christ. *"But now Christ has been raised from the dead, the first fruits of those who are asleep"* (1 Cor. 15:20-21), but also the promise of eternal life for believers through the resurrection and Rapture of the Church.

♦   Jesus Christ fulfills the Feast of Unleavened Bread by overcoming evil. The bread is hidden for three days, as Jesus Christ was hidden in the grave for three days and resurrected on the Festival of First Fruits, *"...every man in his own order: Christ the firstfruits; afterward they that are Christ's at His coming..."*   (I Cor.15:23).

(4)   When a week of weeks (7 weeks; 7 complete Sabbaths; Leviticus 23:15; from the 2nd day of Passover to the day before Shavu'ot equals 49 days or 7 full weeks) have passed after this feast on the 15th day, the Jews celebrated **PENTECOST** on the 50th day (Shavuot or Feast of Weeks); the Shofar (trumpet also known as "Asosra" or "chatzotzera") sounded; 7 lambs were offered as sacrifice; between one Feast of Weeks and the other, and between one New Year and the other, there is an interval of no more than four days [of the week]:

> 1 week = 7 days
> 7 weeks of 7 days = 49 days (The Counting
>   of the Omer)
> (Side note: 50 day journey (47 days plus 3
>   days of separation) from Red Sea to
>   Mount Sinai;
> 50th year is the Year of Jubilee beginning on
>   the Day of Atonement);
> 4 kingdoms would appear and the Messiah
>   would come in the midst of the 4th:

Babylonian, Media-Persian, Greek, and
Roman Empire (Dan 9:24-17)
NOTE: see Daniel's interpretation of
the 70 weeks Daniel 9-10; 7 days =
7 years of Tribulation , 3 1/2 yrs. =
one-half week, occurs after
6,000 years of the time-line
for the last Age.

♦   50 days after Jesus Christ's resurrection the Holy Spirit fell
upon the Apostles in the upper room - Day of Pentecost,
Acts 2:1-13), *"And when the day of Pentecost was fully
come, they were all with one accord in one place..."*
Pentecost means 50 in the Greek—Jesus Christ appeared to
men for 40 days, and the disciples tarried 10 days until the
50th day when Pentecost arrived. From Jesus Christ's birth
through Pentecost began the final countdown to eternity—
the last Age, known as the Age of the Church, a period of
Grace before Judgment.   This is what was meant in
Hebrews 9:26: *"...but now once in the end of the world
hath he appeared to put away sin by the sacrifice of
himself."*   This is an approximate time-period of 2,000
years, and 2,000 years equals one Age. This last Age brings
time, as we know it, to its final culmination—the end of the
6,000 Ages of Time.

♦   *First Trumpet* = Pentecost, the Vernal Equinox has moved
from the stars of Aries to the stars of Pisces.

FALL FESTIVALS
(LATTER RAIN - Hosea 6:3; Joe2:23, James 5:7-8)
MESSIAH'S SECOND COMING

(5)   Feast of **TRUMPETS** (Rosh HaShanah),
Jewish New Year; 1st of "7TH MONTH;" sounding of the
Shofar (ram's horn) to proclaim the ingathering (Leviticus
23:23), *"...you shall have a rest, a reminder by blowing of
trumpets..."*; the fulfillment of the Messianic prophecy; *"For*

the Lord Himself will descend from heaven with a shout...and with the trumpet [shofar] of God; and the dead in Christ shall rise first. Then we who are alive and remain shall be caught up together with them in the clouds (1 Thess. 4:15-17). *"In a moment, in the twinkling of an eye, at the last trump: for the trumpet shall sound, and the dead shall be raised incorruptible, and we shall be changed"* (I Cor 15:52) (see Jewish Wedding).

- According to Josephus, Moses invented the "trumpet" made of silver. It was approximately 1 cubit in length. In a day for a year, 1 cubit = 1,000 years (or interchangeably - a day). The seven trumpets of Revelation equal the 7,000 years of the time-line of Revelation. Moses made two trumpets, one to sound in gathering the heads of the Tribes for consultation and two in gathering the multitude together for Sabbath, festivals, and when the Tabernacle was moved. Two trumpets of 1 cubit (1,000 years) equal 2,000 years which equals "one Age."

- Rosh HaShanah is also known as the "opening of the gates of heaven," and correlates with the 7,000th year, the Millennial or Sabbath rest at the end of the time-line for the Ages. This is a depiction of the resurrection. *"In the seventh month* [the 7,000th year], *in the first day of the month, shall ye have a Sabbath, a memorial of blowing of trumpets, an holy convocation"* (Leviticus 23:24).

- Rosh HaShanah is also known as YOM TERUAH, the Day of the Sounding of the shofar. During the Feast of Trumpets one must not only be listening for (mitzvah), but hear (shema) the awakening blast (Teruah) or sounding of the shofar. *"For the Lord himself shall descend from heaven with a shout, with the voice of the archangel and with the TRUMP (shofar) of God: and the dead in Christ shall rise first"* (I Thessalonians 4:16-17). The frequent blasts of the shofar confuses Satan to prevent him from bringing charges against God's children. He knows his time is at an end because Jesus Christ has come. *"And He shall send His angels with a great sound of a trumpet, and they shall gather together His elect from the four winds, from one end of heaven to another"* (Matthew 24:30,31).

♦ *Last Trumpet* = Rosh HaShanah, the Vernal Equinox has moved from the stars of Pisces to the stars of Aquarius.

(6) **DAY OF ATONEMENT** (Yom Kippur); 10th day of 7th month of Tishri (Leviticus 23:32: a Day of Sabbath Rest); Holiest Day of Jewish Year; High Priest enters Holy of Holies to sprinkle blood on Ark of the Covenant to make atonement for Israel's sins (Leviticus 23:26-32); a Sabbath of complete rest; Second Coming; the Day of Judgment is the future Day of Atonement; Messianic Kingdom; the 7th month; 7 years of tribulation (see Daniel 9:27);

♦ *"For what is our hope, or joy, or crown of rejoicing? Are not even ye in the presence of our Lord Jesus Christ at his coming?"* (I Thess 2:19).

♦ *"For God hath not appointed us to wrath, but to obtain salvation by our Lord Jesus Christ"* (I Thess 5:9). The Day of Atonement (or Judgment) fulfills the Promise that believers in the Messiah, the Church, were not appointed to wrath (or judgment), and thereby completes the Age of the Church. Yom Kippur is also known as the "closing of the gates of heaven."

"And I saw a great white throne, and him that sat on it, from whose face the earth and the heaven fled away; and there was found no place for them. And I saw the dead, small and great, stand before God; and the books were opened: and another book was opened, which is the book of life: and the dead were judged out of those things which were written in the book, according to their works...And whosoever was not found written in the book of life was cast into the lake of fire" (Rev. 20:11-15).

♦ *Great Trump* - Yom Kippur, the Vernal Equinox at the mid-point in the calendar of the stars of Aquarius.

(7) Feast of **TABERNACLES** (Sukkot/Feast of Tabernacles or Booths), 15th day of the 7th month, also known

as Feast of Dedication of the First Temple; rejoiced before the Lord and dwelled for 7 days in "booths" (or 'sukkáhs with at least three sides and an open roof covered by branches/leaves) to remind Israel of their wandering in the wilderness, where God provided shelter, food, and water: *"on the first day shall be a Sabbath, and on the eighth day [Shemini Atzeret] shall be a Sabbath"* (Lev. 23:36-39). The Eighth Day Sabbath is a continuation of the Seventh, a symbol of eternity. The Feast of Tabernacles is a time of provision; 14 lambs (7 x 2) were offered daily along with 70 bulls; blowing of the Shofar with palm branches *"...ye shall celebrate it in the seventh month. Ye shall dwell in booths seven days..."* (Leviticus 23:41-42)— see Jewish Wedding.

"And ye shall take you on the first day the boughs of goodly trees, branches of palm trees, and the boughs of thick trees, and willows of the brook; and ye shall rejoice before the Lord your God seven days." During the Feast of Tabernacles, the yellow citron fruit, date palm branch, myrtle leaves, and willow branches consisting of four species, and representative of the differences in character, are brought together and held as one (in unity; as every nation in the world will come up to Jerusalem to keep the Feast of Tabernacles (Zech. 14:16).   They   are defined as "the upright:" those few who live righteous in deed and thought; "the learned:" those who's deeds have not been refined as the upright, but who understand the law; "the doer of kind deeds:" those who may not be learned, but who are kind, generous, and helpful to others; and "the ordinary:" those who may not possess learning or righteous deeds but who desire to know more. During each day of the Feast of Tabernacles the fruit and branches are waved in all directions (first East, then South, West, North, then up and down).

♦   A similar celebration occurred during Jesus Christ's triumphal entry into Jerusalem recorded in the Gospels of Matthew, Mark, and Luke (see also Zech 9:9). However, this setting of the Gospels occurred a week earlier, during the   Passover,   and   not   the   Feast   of

Tabernacles. Passover (former rain) is symbolic of the First Coming of Jesus Christ, and Tabernacles (latter rain) is symbolic of the Second Coming. The fulfillment of Tabernacles will be at the Second Coming, when Jesus Christ returns in glory to reign in Jerusalem and spread His "tabernacle" over the entire world, *"And I heard a great voice out of heaven saying, Behold, the TABERNACLE of God is with men, and he will DWELL with them, and they shall be his people, and God himself shall be with them, and be their God"* (Rev. 21:3; see also Rev. 7:15).

♦ Even the Gentiles will keep the Feast of Tabernacles: Zechariah 14:16: *"And it shall come to pass that everyone that is left of all the nations which came against Jerusalem shall even go up from year to year to worship the King, the Lord of hosts, and to keep the feast of tabernacles"* (see also Zech. 14:9).

♦ It was during the Feast of Tabernacles where the ceremony of the "pouring of water" occurred when a vase filled with water, known as Mayim Hayim (the Living Water) was taken from the pool of Shiloah. Priests gathered at the Eastern Gate (the same direction Jesus Christ will enter at the Second Coming) waving willow branches from left to right walking toward the city (Isaiah 12:3; Jeremiah 17:12-13; John 7:37-38; Rev 21, Mishnah Sukkot 5:1). A New Testament example of the Feast of Tabernacles is found in John 7: 37-38, when Jesus said, *"In the last day, that great day of the FEAST, Jesus stood and cried, saying, "If any man thirst, let him come unto me, and drink. He that believeth on me, as the scripture hath said, out of his belly shall flow rivers of living water."* In this respect, Jesus was referring to Revelation 21:3 (above) *"the tabernacle of God is with men."*

♦ The Feast of Tabernacles is the celebration of the season of the Messianic Kingdom, *"And God shall wipe away all tears from their eyes; and there shall be no more death, neither sorrow, nor crying, neither shall there be any more pain: for the former things are passed away...And he said unto me, It is done. I am Alpha and Omega, the beginning and the end. I will give unto him that is athirst of the fountain of the water of life freely"* (Rev. 21:4-6).

♦ The 7,000 year as the Messianic Kingdom can be further referenced in Zechariah 3:8-9, *"...behold, I will bring forth my servant the BRANCH* [the Messiah]. *For behold the stone that I have laid before Joshua, upon one stone shall be seven eyes* [7,000 years]*..."* (see also Zech. 4:2; Dan. 2:44-45).

FROM THE KING JAMES BIBLE 1611/1830

According to Josephus (Book III), *"...this proportion of the measures of the tabernacle proved to be an imitation of the system of the world: for that third part thereof was within the four pillars, to which the priests were not admitted, is, as it were, a heaven peculiar to God."*

CHAPTER II

A PATTERN OF THE TRUE

What is a "pattern?" A pattern is a design or mold depicting "the original," "the ideal," or the "figure of the true." You might say the same of "symbolism." Symbolism may be a way to pattern after a figure of the true. Augustine believed this also when he wrote, *"...the important thing is to consider the significance of a fact and not to dispute its authenticity." (5)* And if there be a "true picture" what representation is the Book of Revelation's symbolism patterned after?

As revealed in Chapter I, the tabernacle of Moses was a likeness of the Throne of God in the heavens *"which are the figures of the true..."* (Heb 9:23), and yet the tabernacle was a pattern of things to come (Heb 8:5; 9, 10)—prophecy. Prophecy reveals the truth of the future: *"Who* [priests of the tabernacle] *serve unto the example and shadow of heavenly things, as Moses was admonished of God when he was about to make the tabernacle: for, See, saith he, that thou make all things according to the PATTERN shewed to thee in the mount."*

The Book of Revelation, like Moses' tabernacle, depicts a future, symbolic imagery of this same tabernacle in the wilderness only now depicted in the heavens. *"Now of the things which we have spoken this is the sum: We have such an high priest* [Jesus Christ]*, who is set on the right hand of the throne of the Majesty in the heavens; A minister of the* *sanctuary and of the true tabernacle, which the Lord pitched, and not man"* (Heb. 8:1-2).

Obviously, the Book of Revelation was mysteriously symbolic. This was due largely to the great persecution endured by the early Christians. After Rome virtually drove Christianity underground, Christians began to utilize (among other symbolic representations) the sacred, pagan symbols of the Graeco-Romans to express their worship of the Most High and to disguise their true worship of Jesus Christ. For this reason, much of prophecy is clothed in astronomical symbolism depicting a prophetic time-period encompassing the historical background and future outlook for the Church and the Jewish people.

The Greek word describing the Book of Revelation is "Apokalypsis or Apocalypse," a combination of the Greek kalupto, which means "unveiling," and apo, meaning "from." When something is unveiled it is revealed, uncovered, unfolded, unsealed, or disclosed. It is a way of letting someone in on a secret, exposing what was once previously hidden now laid open and brought to light—all things in relation to heaven must be revealed. It is the parting of the curtain, the rendering of the "veil," or the Revelation of the One Who is the High Priest, *"Having, therefore, brethren, boldness to enter into the holiest by the blood of Jesus, By a new and living way, which he hath consecrated for us, THROUGH THE VEIL, that is to say, HIS FLESH"* (Heb. 10:19-20).

This is a way of letting the reader know that "symbolism" is merely a way of disguising the truth from the profane or unbeliever. Because the Book of Revelation contains the Revelation of Jesus Christ, only those who have accepted Him as Lord and Savior can clearly understand the Revelation—it is a book of "prophetic" insight and can only be discerned through the Power of the Holy Spirit. Deuteronomy 29:29 describes this well, *"...the secret things belong unto the Lord our God; but those things which are revealed belong unto us and to our children forever."*

Through a time-span covering thousands of years, the Book of Revelation reveals time-periods that mark various periods in history as well as the New Testament Church by condensing the dispensations of the Gospel into Seven (7) Church "Ages." In writing, *"the time is at hand"* (Rev. 1:3), John gives the urgency behind the study of this book, because surely as even more time passes, the days of the complete fulfillment of this book draw closer.

The Seven Churches

The 7,000 year time-line was referenced as early as A.D. 300 by the Bishop of Pettau, a martyr in the cause of Christ. It was also mentioned by a few other notables including the Epistle of Barnabas (15:3-4), the Book of Enoch, and Josephus (Antiquities), but the understanding of what exactly constitutes an "Age" in light of the 7,000 year time-line of Revelation and how it is presented throughout Scripture is new to this modern-age and never before presented similarly in light of prophecy. All that was previously known of this original time-line has been lost to antiquity, even among the early Greeks and Egyptians, who transformed it into occultic teachings and pseudo-sciences such as astrology. In these latter days, though, it seems appropriate that God has resurrected the remnants of this knowledge for all to know the urgency of the time at hand, and the record has been preserved in the Bible.

The Seven Churches of Ephesus, Smyrna, Pergamos, Thyatira, Sardis, Philadelphia, and Laodicea were located in a relatively small portion of Asia Minor along with the Churches at Colosse, Hierapolis, Miletus (near the Isle of Patmos), and Troas (Acts 20:17-38; Col 1:2; 2 Tim 4:20), and included the Christians of Bithynia, Pontus, Galatia, and Cappadocia (I Peter 1:1).

Although there were more than Seven Churches in all of Asia, in the beginning chapters of the Book of Revelation, it would appear John writes to and for the benefit of Seven specific Churches (1:4). The events foretold in the Book of Revelation pass far beyond the life time of those who dwelt in the earliest of these Christian cities; yet, they are compared to the seven candlesticks contained in the Holy Place of the Sanctuary.

Why were the Churches described with heavenly symbolism of angels and stars? Remember, John writes of the "earthly" tabernacle in comparison to the heavenly one. The earthly tabernacle contained the two areas, one being the Holy Place with the seven candlesticks (lampstands) and the other the Most Holy Place of the Most High God. Now picture the heavenly tabernacle amongst the stars of heaven. The candlesticks would be located in the universe represented by the "seven" then known planets in the heavens. In the "midst" of the seven candlesticks was *"one like unto the Son of man"* (vs. 13). He is depicted *"clothed with a garment down to the foot, and girt about the paps with a golden girdle. His head and his hairs were white like wool, as white as snow and his eyes were as a flame of fire"* (vs. 13-14).

Verses 13-14 appear as a description of the "sun." Verse 16 tells us this comparison is correct: *"...and his countenance was as the sun shineth in his strength."* John compares the Son of Man in His strength and centralized position within the heavenly sanctuary to the similar attributes of the "sun" as the center of the universe. This same reference can be found in Matthew 17:1-13, *"And His countenance was as the sun shineth in its strength...and His face did shine as the sun, and His raiment was white as the light...."*

Without the light of the sun, the reflection of sunlight upon the moon, and the glittering stars in the heavens, the universe would be a very dark place. Here again, the Light of the Son of God is compared to the light emitted by the sun in our universe, *"And the city* [New Jerusalem] *had no need of the sun, neither of the moon, to shine in it: for the glory of God did lighten it..."* (Rev. 21:23).

More importantly, Jesus Christ is represented in the center of the candlesticks as the Light, whereas in the early sanctuary there was only the candlesticks present—which further proves His fulfillment as High Priest of the sanctuary of heaven, and the coming Meshiach ben David, the Conquering King.

Paul writes in Ephesians 1:20-21, that Jesus Christ has been set at the right hand of God in the heavenly places, *"...far above all principality, and power, and might, and dominion, and every name that is named, not only in this world, but also in that which is to come."* Now this brings up something rather interesting: For hundreds of years, ancient astronomers thought the "earth" was the center of the universe, not the "sun." Interesting isn't it? Early science needed to learn the astronomy of the Book of Revelation, and it would have made the discovery much sooner.

But again, why only "seven" candlesticks and "seven" angels? Could this reference to Seven Churches encompass the entirety of the gospel in seven periods of "time or Ages?" The number seven denotes completion or fullness, a sacred number, and if used in connotation with the seven Church Ages represents the fullness or completion of the gospel work. It represents the time of the Gentile Church in its fullness, and the culmination of the gospel being preached to all of the world from the time of the Apostles to the close of the "Ages."

The Seven Churches reveal a capsulated version of the entire 7,000 year time-span from Adam but condensed into one "Age" of 2,000 years. The symbols and imagery describing certain events in history correlate with the seven Ages of the Church and harmonize with other parts of Scripture for various time-periods. Most importantly, future events might be described as one continuous and successive occurrence even though they could be thousands of years apart—this is a good explanation of prophecy, and described perfectly in Rev. 1:19, when the Messiah explained to John: *"Write the things which thou hast seen, and the things which are, and the things which shall be hereafter."*

John describes the current events of the Church based upon the historical base of the Jewish people, and prophetically looks forward into the future describing the various stages of Church growth, persecution, strife, heresies, anti-christ doctrinal influences, catching away, Second Coming, Millennium, Judgment, the New Jerusalem, and God's plan for the Jewish people—all of this in Seven Church Ages.

Understanding Revelation's Sabbath Rest

In order to compile all of the prophetic time-periods, it also becomes vitally important to understand the revelation of the truth of the Holy Sabbath (Shabbat/Shabbat kodesh), and the word Sabbath, means "rest" (Hebrew 4:8).   God has sanctified the Sabbath because the Sabbath has and always will be associated with the "seventh" day (Genesis 2:1-3) when God ceased from His works. The Seventh Day of the Sabbath Rest stands for the day of completion. The Seventh Day is also described in relationship to the 1,000 years of the Millennial "rest" for the Christian Church (see Psalm 90:4), and clearly evident in Isaiah 66:22-23, in describing the new heavens and earth: *"For as the new heavens and the new earth, which I will make, shall remain before me...And it shall come to pass, that from one new moon to another, and from one sabbath to another, shall all flesh come to worship before me, saith the Lord."*

This is vitally important to comprehend in relationship to God's timetable for the Ages, and this calculation of time will never deviate from Genesis to Revelation, as expressed in Ecclesiastes, *"I know that whatsoever God doeth, it shall be for ever...(3:14-15).*   Remember, Jesus Christ is the *"Alpha and Omega, the beginning and the end, the first and the last"* (Rev. 22:13), and *"...the same yesterday, and today, and for ever"* (Heb 13:8).

This means that the consistency of God's Word can be relied upon to be Truth. Therefore, the time-periods of the Bible, including the 1,000 to 7,000th year time-line, can also be depended upon, as the Apostle Peter wrote, *"But, beloved, be not ignorant of this one thing, that one day is with the Lord as a thousand years, and a thousand years as one day"* (II Peter 3:8; also see Num 14:32-34 and Ezek 4:2-5). This reference can be rather confusing unless you understand God's time-line for the Ages in accordance with the Sabbath rest.

"Rest" (in Hebrew m'nuchah), therefore, is something we "enter into and remain" (see Isaiah 11:10).   It occurs in relation to a certain time period (i.e., 7,000 years) or day of the week (7th day), but also into a much farther, indefinite period known as "eternity." The Day of Rest is also a future period of time spoken of in Hebrews, *"There remaineth therefore a rest to the people of God"* (Hebrews 4:9). Here again, one can find the principle of the seventh day rest in *"For we which have believed do enter into rest, as he said, As I have sworn in my wrath, if they shall enter into my rest: although the works were finished from the foundation of the world"* (vs:3).

The plan of God's rest was instituted from the foundations of the world beginning in Genesis through its culmination in the Book of Revelation: But there is another Day of Rest in the future, *"And in this place again, If they shall enter into my rest...Let us labour therefore to enter into that rest..."* (vs 5-11), and this occurs at the end of God's timetable for mankind (also known as the Day of the Lord or as John wrote in the beginning of Revelation, "the Lord's Day").

If someone asks, "...but Jesus rose from the dead on Sunday, the eighth day of the week. Shouldn't that day be the Sabbath?"—The important thing to remember is that Jesus Christ fulfilled the Sabbath rest. *"The Son of man is Lord also of the Sabbath"* (Mark 2:27; Matthew 12:8). He has entered into the Sabbath rest, just as we enter into Him, *"Come unto Me, all ye that labour and are heavy laden, and I will give you rest...Take my yoke upon you, and learn of Me...and ye shall find rest unto your souls."* (Matthew 11:28, 29). It is not the law of keeping of the Sabbath on Saturday or worshipping on Sunday, as in the day, but that our souls' find eternal rest in the One Who has fulfilled the Sabbath (see Isaiah 28:8-12). The Seventh Day will forever be known as the

Sabbath—nothing in the Word of God has changed this fact. The Seventh Day Sabbath is the true Sabbath, passing beyond the earthly observance to the spiritual and continuing on without interruption throughout eternity.

The Eighth Day, also known as "the day of lingering," means to continue or remain in God's presence or rest. The Eighth Day is also known as Shimchat Torah, a picture of the end of the Ages, the Millennial rest, and the final judgment, or Bema Judgement. The Eighth Day is merely a continuation of the Seventh Day similarly as the eight days of Passover carry over into the first day of the Feast of Unleavened Bread and Festival of Firstfruits. This can be seen in the example of when Jesus Christ rose from the dead *"...and became the firstfruits of them that slept"* (1 Cor 15:20).

So what was John referring to when he wrote, *"I was in the Spirit on the Lord's Day"* (1:10). The Lord's day means the Sabbath Day. Remember, John was writing of a future, prophetic time period, but he also sanctioned the only day that could be called the Lord's day, — *"...the hour cometh, when ye shall neither in this mountain, nor yet at Jerusalem, worship the Father...."* What hour? The hour when the *"true worshippers shall worship the Father in spirit and in truth..."* because *"...God is a Spirit: and they that worship him must worship him in spirit and in truth"* (John 4:21-24).

For this reason, throughout the Book of Revelation, all prophecy ends on the "seventh" day as a symbol for completion and eternity. John was clearly referencing the Sabbath Day rest—the compilation of the entire Church Age as seen in the depiction of the Seven Churches.

A Beginning Revelation

In the beginning chapters of Revelation, John was carried into the Spirit, therefore, he was viewing time in light of the Holy Spirit's revelation. According to the Holy Spirit, John was to *"Write the things which thou hast seen, and the things which are, and the things which shall be hereafter"* (1:19).

And then John heard behind him *"...a great voice, as of a trumpet"* (1:10). Trumpets' proclaim   prophetic messages clearly *announcing* God's intervention in time to reveal a specific event in history. The sound of the first trumpet (an alarm, a wake-up call) was to announce a specific time-period, and this was a proclamation and introduction to the Age of the Gospel of Jesus Christ represented by the Seven Churches depicted in seven, distinct periods of history, and these would be known as "Church Ages." The Church Ages align with the seven most Holiest of the Jewish Feasts (covered in an earlier chapter). The Jewish Feasts align with God's timetable, and God's time-table aligns with the movements of the heavens.

Heaven is precise, but unfortunately, our calculation of time can be a source of great confusion, and if you were to undertake a study on the origins of various calendar systems, it would be quite obvious why mankind's timetable is very "unexact."   Everyone knows that clocks in different places register time differently. The time-line in Genesis 1 or in Exodus 20:11, is based upon man's understanding of time in the six ordinary days of Creation? God views time from the beginning to the end (Is. 46:10; Rev 22:13; Job 8:58). He is, therefore, not regulated by the same parameters as earth but stands outside of time. Time is merely an element of Creation, a feature of His universe, similar to the composition of the elements, space, and time. God's purpose in defining time was to define it in relationship to the earth's rotation and motion around the sun, and by doing so, defined time in periods relative to our own frame of reference (Genesis 1:5, 14-15).

CHAPTER III

A CALENDAR FOR EARTH

Augustine once wrote, *"I heard from a learned man that the motions of the sun, moon, and stars constituted time."* He then prefaced his statement with, *"...but if I wish to explain it to one who asks, I know not."*

Augustine was among the majority of people facing this dilemma. Most people today are so familiar with their faithful watch, ticking away day after day, and pulling the sheets off of their daily calendar, they never even think about how, where, or when this system of Time began. Questions about what constitutes Time have been the subject and focus of hundreds of books on theory, philosophy, and even religion; but where science has failed to examine, "prophecy" has taken up the cause.

The forerunners to the ancient study of Time were always watchers of the sky, "aster" (star) "onomers" (observers of the heavens), and even the ancient prophets all studied the movements of the heavens as they foretold the Creator's calendar and timetable for mankind. It would be safe to conclude that wherever you read of prophecy in the Bible, the prophecy is always associated with Time, and time-lines always evolve around God's timetable. Once this time-line is understood, everything else, including prophecy, will harmonize.

Up to this point, it should be evident how the 7,000 year time-line can be found throughout the Bible broken down into seven 1,000 year subdivisions from the time of Adam to the End of the Ages.   It can be seen in Moses' tabernacle in the wilderness reflecting the heavenly sanctuary, in the Feast Days and how they coincide with the First and Second Coming of the Messiah, and also   found in the Book of Revelation.   In following along with Augustine's thought, the next question should be, "It's in the Bible, but what exactly is it?"

For over a thousand years, from approximately A.D. 200 to 1500, great attempts were made to establish a record of prior history that aligned with fixed dates.   During this time-period, calendar systems underwent great transitions in efforts to resolve muddled, conflicting, and confusing dates.   The early Reformers thought the Church purposely intended to change the calendar to confuse the time of the rapture.   Nevertheless, amidst the loud protests and resulting riots, the numerous problems surrounding the calendar were put to rest by Pope Gregory XIII, in A.D. 1582, when he adopted the use of the Gregorian calendar as the standard for the measurement of time.

As a result, as it stands today, the Holy Bible gives us a good estimation of time-periods, but precise dates prior to A.D. 500 are difficult to determine. Most historical dates were based upon estimated time-periods calculated from the lives of early Biblical patriarchs such as Moses, Abraham, and the prophets. Obviously, if precise dates were known then the exact day and year of Jesus Christ's birth would be known, which now can only be approximated, and everyone would be scurrying to be ready for the exact date of Jesus Christ's return. Perhaps, this reveals the wisdom of God, in that no person knows exactly the hour of Christ's return, only the "season."

God's time-clock aligns with the movements of the heavens, and the heavens determine the seasons. For instance, if someone on the East coast observed the constellation of Aries on the Western horizon early in the evening, they would have a fairly   good   idea   that   the   Spring   Equinox   was   near.

Unfortunately, through the thousands of years in the development of the calendar, far too many variations of a simple system has brought a world of confusion and changes, for example consider the following calendars: lunar/solar (equinoctial and/or tropical, or sidereal), Macedonian, Julian, Talmudic, Civil Year, Sacred Year, International Fixed, World, Gregorian and a few others not mentioned. Also, depending on the interpretation, there can be a "sidereal day," "apparent solar day," "mean solar day," "civil day," or "ecclesiastical day." Days can be measured from sunrise to sunset, sunset to sunset, sunrise to sunrise, from noon to noon.

If the various calendar systems were all created the same, time-periods wouldn't be all that difficult to understand. Therefore, it is very important not to get too confused over "seasons" and "days" or "hours," and for this reason an understanding of "Ages" can be relatively accurate, but definitely not precise.

The simple system currently used today revolves around a 24 hour day comprised of a circle with 60 minutes containing 60 seconds. **"...And the evening and the morning"** (Genesis 1). Today, we, thankfully, use clocks. A clock is basically a device for calculating the movements of the heavens, because the same face on modern-day clocks can be found in the placement of the heavens as the marking of the Ages of Mankind. An age is simply a period of measured "time" just like the face of your clock depicts the time of day.

According to the Bible, the counterfeit of the true measurement of time and the calendar of the heavens is Satan's great deception: astrology.

The Early Hebrews' Time Clock

The early Hebrew scholar, Maimonides, indicates the feasts of the Hebrews were sanctified not by a calendar, but by the heavens and regulated by the moon. It was a far advanced, yet simplistic, observation of the new moon and its cycles. The beginning of the year began with the "New Moon" (Rosh

Chodesh, first of the month) nearest the equinox. Accordingly, the Jewish months of the calendar were restructured and conformed to the ideas and the symbolism to align with Jewish traditions. The Hebrew calendar (yereah), also consisting of lunar months (chodesh), a solar year (shanah), and the 13th intercalary month of Adar, begins with the proposed date of Creation, October 7, 3761 B.C.E. (the month of Thisri). In September of 1999, the Hebrew year will be 5760 based upon B.C.E. 3761. In contrast, according to the King James Bible (1611/1826), the Christian calculation for the current Age began with B.C.E. 4,000.

In the calendar of the heavens, the first month of the Jewish religious year begins with Nisan 1, corresponding to the Vernal (or Spring) Equinox. During Abraham's lifetime, the Vernal Equinox could be seen among the stars in the constellation of Taurus, known as "the bull of heaven."

The heavens move constantly, and the Vernal Equinox remains in one constellation for approximately 2,000 years before moving to the next. After 2,000 years, the Vernal Equinox moved from the stars of Taurus to the constellation of Aries. At the same time the Hebrew calendar changed from the Civil year to the Religious Year. NOTE: For the most part, only the Latin (and sometimes Arabic) names of the constellations are used today. These are not the same names the Hebrews used thousands of years ago. The Hebrew root for some of the more important constellations will be included later.

The current Jewish calendar was established by Hillel II in B.C.E. 360, and so Aviv (Nisan) correlates to April, the stars of Aries, and changed to the 1st month according to Exodus 12:1-2, while Tishri moved to the 7th month. The movement of the Equinox is how the early Hebrews (along with the New Moon) resolved their calendar. This movement of the Equinox is called "The Precession of the Equinox" (PE) which will be covered in-depth later. Briefly, the PE more than any other system follows God's time-clock, and this system follows the original, true calendar given to mankind. This can be seen in the way the Precession of the Equinox follows the 7,000 year time-line from Adam to the End of the Ages.

An example of this would be when the PE moved from Aries (April, Aviv) to Pisces, and this occurred at the same time that Jesus Christ came to this earth as a babe. This was the beginning of the 2,000-year Age of the Church. At the Second Coming, the PE will have moved out of Pisces and into Aquarius; thus,— as New Agers have borrowed the phrase— begins the Age of Aquarius and according to God's timetable, the Second Coming. (The corruption of the PE evolved into the worship of the seasons).

Another way to look at this would be that during the life of Abraham the "civil calendar" was used predominantly, and with the Exodus from Egypt and the first Passover Lamb, a new religious calendar emerged. This calendar, ordained by God, began in the Spring with the month of Nisan (Aviv), and according to Josephus when the sun was in Aries (Ex. 12:2). The religious calendar begins in the Jewish calendar in the Spring (seen as the former rain, the First Coming of the Messiah in the New Testament) and the Civil Calendar begins in the Fall (seen as the latter rain, the Second Coming)— exactly "6" months apart. The former and latter rain can also be seen in the beginning chapters of Luke with the birth of John the Baptist "6" months earlier than Jesus Christ (Luke 1:24,26,36,56). It is a process of repetition throughout the Bible, and can be seen evidenced in the two Jewish calendar systems being "6" months apart.

After reading the first words of Genesis, *"In the beginning...,"* it should be easily understood that God established "time" with its seasons, hours, days, and minutes. Calculating the seasons is very scriptural (see Genesis 1:14), because all throughout the Bible one can read the various time-periods and seasons of very important prophecies. Wisdom precludes that no person knows the "day" or "hour" of the Messiah's return, but likewise, God has given us the "age" or "season" of His return (Mark 13:21). Just as the clock tells us what time it is!   When the clock strikes 12:00, we know it is either noon or midnight.   For example, Herod knew in advance of the coming of the birth of the Messiah—he didn't know the day or the hour, just the general time-period; and Paul tells believers they will not be "surprised" at Jesus Christ's return, only nonbelievers (1 Thess 5:4).

Throughout scripture God has told His people what He is going to do ahead of time--that's prophecy. For example, look at the life of Noah. Noah was told in advance of the Great Flood, and even as the rains were about to come pouring down, God gave Noah "SEVEN" days notice in advance (Genesis 7:4). This is another picture of the 7,000 year time-line.   Jesus Christ revealed that His Second Coming would be like the days of Noah (Matthew 24:37).   Just like in the Age of Noah, the unbelieving were caught by surprise, but God told Noah, as He has His people, far in advance of His Coming.   The end of the Age was determined even before Moses' wilderness tabernacle and known by the early Hebrews as Athid Lavo, The Coming Age.

Understanding the Time-Line of Abraham

Sir Wm. Drummond studied ancient sky-watchers and described them as mysterious ancient ones who lived much earlier than recorded history.

"The fact is certain, that at some remote period, there were mathematicians and astronomers who knew that the sun is in the centre of our system, and that the earth, itself a planet, revolved round the central fire; who attempted to calculate the return of comets' who indicated the number of solar years contained in the great cycle...and fixed with considerable accuracy the distance of the Moon and the circumference of the earth; who held that the face of the Moon was diversified with valleys and seas; who asserted that there was a planet beyond Saturn; who reckoned the planets to be sixteen in number; and who calculated the length of the tropical year within three minutes of the true time." (6)

These ancient ones referenced by Drummond were those descending out of the Ark from the Great Flood and who passed on their ancient astronomical knowledge through the early patriarchs. This knowledge came to future generations as the astronomy of Abraham.

The process from Genesis to Revelation, from the Beginning to the End, can be found in the time periods known as "Ages." For instance, in Hebrews 1:2, *"by whom also he made the worlds. "*—worlds should be correctly translated from the Greek as "Ages." This same reference can also be found in Chapter 11:3, *"...the worlds were framed by the word of God."* Worlds, here again, should be translated as "Ages or universe." Josephus explains this time period of Ages as being marked by the recording of history, and Jewish recorded history, according to Josephus, began around the time of Abram (Abraham), *"...before the time of Abraham, real truth is so strangely blended with apparent, that little reliance can be placed on the various traditionary accounts of earlier events"* (7).

And with the recording of history, two approaches to the study of the heavens (attempted) to part ways: the worship of the heavens through astrology and the study of the heavens through astronomy. Unfortunately, idolatry would always be a continued source of temptation for the people of God. It was the Chaldeans and Mesopotamians who brought with them from Babylon the worship of many gods of the heavens (astrology), but it was Abraham's worship of one God that resulted in his persecution and separation. For this reason, God led Abraham out of the land above Babylon and brought him into the land of Canaan (Judea).

The time-line of Abraham was handed down from Noah, passed down through the various nations that settled upon the earth, and interpreted in various methods from astrology to astronomy. Abraham gave his knowledge of astronomy to the Egyptians, who had already obtained a rudimentary study of the heavens borrowed from the Babylonians, and the Egyptians then passed their knowledge of the heavens to the Greeks.

Basically, early civilizations' calculated the heavens in 12 time-periods of 360 days equaling one year. The same 360 degrees that measure the circumference of a circle. A good example of this can be found in the Old Testament passage in II Kings 20:8-11 which aligns with the 7,000 year time-line for the End of the Age. *"And Hezekiah said unto Isaiah, 'What shall be the sign that the Lord will heal me, and that I shall go up into the third day?' And Isaiah said, 'This sign shalt thou have of the Lord, that the Lord will do the thing that he hath spoken: shall the shadow go forward ten degrees, or go back ten degrees?'"*

If you divide the 360 degree circumference of circle by 12 months of the year (or constellations), the answer is 30. There are 30 degrees in each of the 12 star constellations. One-tenth or 1/10 of the 30 degrees is 10 degrees (see also Ezek. 41:5-6).

Today, this calculation of time in II Kings is known as the Precession of the Equinox or PE. The PE was known to Abraham, but officially not recognized until approximately B.C.E. 150 by Hipparchus. It was Moses who passed this precise calculation down through history, because the wilderness tabernacle, the Jewish feast days, and eventually the calendar all align with the PE. God gave Moses (Ex 12) this knowledge when He changed the Jewish Calendar to align with the PE. This happened when the PE moved from the stars in the constellation of Taurus into the stars of Aries, during the spring, known to the Hebrews as Aviv or Nisan.

What Exactly is the Precession of the Equinox?

Hebrew is read from right to left the same way the Precession of the Equinox (PE) reads from right to left. The PE moves counterclockwise in the heavens, just like the hands on the face of a clock. In fact, if you picture the face of a clock as an example, the PE could be very easily understood. The earth spins very slowly toward the east which results in a rotation of the celestial sphere toward the west.

In order to fully understand the PE, it's important to understand the Earth's movement. The "apparent" path of the sun is known as the ecliptic, which remains in a stationary position, but the equator moves, and when the sun crosses the equator it becomes known as the Equinox. The two points where the ecliptic and equator meet determine our seasons. Keep in mind also, this is based on the "apparent" path of the sun. By apparent it means as if the sun looked to be moving, but in actuality the sun stands still while the earth revolves around the sun.

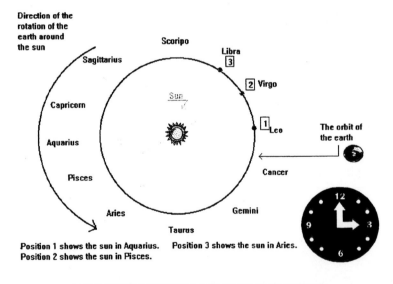

Position 1 shows the sun in Aquarius.   Position 3 shows the sun in Aries.
Position 2 shows the sun in Pisces.

THE PRECESSION OF THE EQUINOX

The Bible contains an enormous amount of astronomy plus just plain, practical wisdom. The early patriarchs knew of the PE, it existed from Creation. The Bible clearly indicates the sun as the center of the universe, but science needed to catch up, too. It wasn't until much later in history when sky observers fully recognized the "sun" (not the earth) as the center of the universe.

The change in seasons is due to the ecliptic, and this is how the four seasons came to be named:

Vernal (or Spring) Equinox: the sun crosses the equator while traveling north; day and night are equal in length = Spring

Autumnal Equinox: the sun crosses the equator while traveling to the south, day and night are equal in length = Autumn

Summer and winter were determined by the position of the Solstice points. Solstice means "standing of the Sun." The Solstice points were located 90 degrees from the Equinox, and this was the point where the sun appeared to "stand still" before reversing its northward or southward direction.

Summer Solstice: the sun travels north, longer days and shorter nights; longest day

Winter Solstice: the sun reaches its farthest point to the south; longer nights and shorter days; shortest day

On either side of the ecliptic is an imaginary belt containing eight degrees (16 total), and this belt contains the apparent path of the sun, also the moon and the five, then known, planets: Mercury, Venus, Mars, Jupiter, and Saturn.

If you look at the face of a clock again, you would observe the same circular pattern in the heavens containing the 12 star constellations. Each one of the 12 constellations are further divided into 30 degree sections, and if you multiply 12 times 30 the sum is 360 days (also known as degrees). With a few revisions, this is basically how we derived our calendar system today. Although, the Jewish year uses a calculation of 354.36 days with one month (Ve-Adar, a leap month) occurring 7 times every 19 years.

The usual order of the constellations begins with the sun in the stars of Aries and moves counterclockwise ending with the constellation Pisces (eastwardly) while the PE moves in the opposite direction (westwardly). Today, the PE has moved clockwise around the circle through the constellation near the point of zero degrees of Aquarius. When the PE arrives at the zero degree of Aquarius, it will be known as a different Age, hence the term "Age of Aquarius."

This phrase, "Age of Aquarius," should have a familiar ring from astrology, but actually the concept (not the name) originates from Biblical cosmology. As a note: astrologers, for the most part, erroneously continue to use Aries as the first sign. If not for Biblical reasons alone, it is totally inaccurate to follow birth signs today, because the PE has moved almost three signs through the constellations.

Today, we know it takes roughly 2,000 (2,154 years to be exact) for the PE to move through one star constellation measuring 30 degrees, and approximately 25,000 (25,848 years to be exact) for the PE to move through each one of the 12 divisions of the 360 degree circle before returning to its original point of calculation. The ancient patriarchs rounded this 2,154 number to an approximate number of 2,000. Ecclesiates 8:5, reads, **"...a wise man's heart discerneth both time and judgment."** This 2,000 year time-period is called an "Age."

The path of the Vernal Equinox depicts the "Ages" in 2,000 year increments. In other words, as an example, on the face of a clock it takes 15 minutes (3 x 5 min intervals) to equal 1/4 of the hour. In determining Ages it takes 3 Ages of 2,000 years to equal 6,000 years. The Covenant of Abraham begins in the Age of Taurus and ends 6,000 years later at the beginning point of the Age of Aquarius.

Modern Biblical scholars, puzzled over the meaning of an Age, fail to understand the word in the context of Scripture. For instance, in Greek, Matthew 28:20, Hebrews 1:2, and 11:3, interpret the word "universe" as periods of "time or ages," and this period of time began with "age" of Adam. The early Jewish historian, Josephus, in his writings often refer to the "Age" of Noah. The Age of Noah is associated with a time period or "season" and would be correlated with the time of the Great Flood.

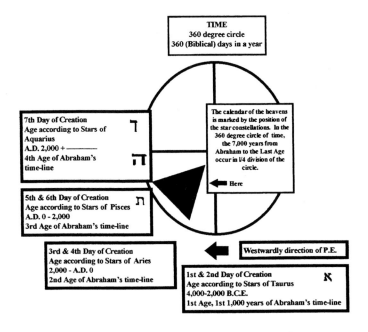

**PATH OF THE VERNAL EQUINOX
AGES OF TIME**

    The ancients also configured into their calculations
another time-period of 1,000 years (Mizmor, see Psalm 90:4),
as explained in Chapter 1. This is also what the Apostle Peter
made reference to in II Peter 3:8, *"But, beloved, be not
ignorant of this one thing, that one day is with the Lord as a
thousand years, and a thousand years as one day."* This
reference can be rather confusing unless you understand God's
time-line for the Ages, but Peter was referring to the various
"Ages" of mankind from the Age of Creation, the Age of Noah,
through the Age of Judgment and the Age of the New Heavens
and Earth.

A picture of the Ages can be seen in Genesis 6:3, when the Lord said, *"My spirit shall not always strive with man, for that he also* [is] *flesh: yet his days shall be an hundred and twenty years."* This passage of Scripture reveals the time-line of the Ages. Genesis 6:3 refers not only to the length of years in a man's life (as 120 years old), but that the Ages of man shall be 120 years. The entire time-period allotted for mankind. This can be explained further in understanding the year of Jubilee every 50 years, a year of rest. Multiply 120 years of Ages times 50 years of Jubilee and the result is 6,000 years.

The last Age is the Seventh Day, or Sabbath rest equating to the 7,000 year (a day for a year). Hosea 6:1-2 concurs with II Peter 3:8, where each day is rightly understood to mean a 1000 years, *"Come, let us return to the Lord. For he has torn us, but He will heal us; he has wounded us, but He will bandage us. He will revive us after two days; He will raise us up on the third day that we may live before Him."*

This calculation can be easily defined as: 2 days equal two periods of 1,000 years or 2,000 years, and 3 days x 2,000 years (1,000 years x 2 Ages) = 6,000 years.

The Six Ages from Abraham

In the Old Testament whenever God appeared to his people, He always came with "clouds" (Ex. 13:21, 40:34-38; Luke 9:35). In the same way Jesus Christ ascended in the clouds after His resurrection (Acts 1:9), He will also descend "with and in" the clouds at His Second Coming (Rev. 1:7, Matt. 24:30).

Again as a reminder, this is not a study on numerology, astrology, etc., but the way God originally intended the use of the heavens; namely, as a giant, heavenly clock, a time-piece revealing the Centuries from beginning to end, and the clock is fast winding down to the "End of the Age." Continue to think of "Ages" in alignment with the constellations rather than as they were later corrupted as in the practice of astrology.

The calculation of the "Ages" began with the star constellation located at the Vernal Equinox. As determined earlier, prior to Moses and the children of Israel's Exodus from Egypt, the Vernal Equinox was situated in the constellation of Taurus during Abraham's lifetime.   Revelation 1:7, reads in speaking of Jesus Christ (in the Greek), *"I am Al'-pha and O-me'ga, the beginning and the ending."*   The word "alphabet" comes from the first letter of the Jewish alphabet, Aleph, א

and where the word, elephant, originated. Elephant, meaning "strong." Aleph also means 'thousand," ox, bull, strength, leader, teach, and "first." This is when the Father made a Covenant with Abraham, and also represents one of the "four" principal banners of the 12 tribes of Israel.

Another association of Aleph in Scripture is found in Habakkuk 3:3, where God's power over the universe is compared to "light," "horns" (as in the bull, Taurus, Aleph), and representing power: *"His glory covered the heavens, and the earth was full of his praise, And his brightness was as the light; he had horns coming out of his hand and there was the hiding of his power."*

The root word, Aleph, is found on the previous picture of the Path of the Equinox describing the "FIRST" Age of two "THOUSAND" years This would be during the Age of Taurus, because the Age of Taurus marks the beginning point of the Vernal Equinox from the time of Creation to Abraham (B.C.E. 4,000-2,000).

The next Age would be calculated from Moses (the wilderness sanctuary), to the time of the Messiah (B.C.E. 2,000-using 0 A.D.). Remember, in Exodus 12, when God changed the religious calendar to Aviv (Nisan). This was to correct the time-period to the true Equinox time (as Hebrew is read from right to left) marked by the constellation of Aries. The value of the Hebrew letter is increased to 1,000 times its ordinary value when it is written LARGE = thus, Aleph (meaning Abba, Father) is counted as 1000. So the Aleph on the time-clock represents 1,000 and the beginning point of the counting down of the Ages.

Again, looking at the face of a clock, the Age of Taurus would position the minutes hand at half past the hour to coincide with the PE and the Vernal (or spring) Equinox. The depiction of the PE beginning with the spring festivals (Age of Taurus) can be seen in the ancient Jewish betrothal of the bride and groom, and will culminate in the wedding as seen in the fall festivals (Age of Aquarius) (this will be covered later).

The time-line of Abraham coincides with 6,000 years of 3 Ages x 2,000 years. The Covenant of Abraham begins in the Age of Taurus, at the Aleph, and ends 6,000 years later with the A g e   of Pisces. The Hebrew root for the Age of Pisces is: Tav ת

Tav is the last letter of the Hebrew alphabet marking the last Age of the 6,000 year time-line. Interestingly, in Hebrew, Tav means sign, mark, the last, a cross, covenant, or seal.

The Book of Revelation compresses all of the Ages as a pictorial view of the time-clock during the Piscean Age which includes all "six" Ages of the Church mentioned in the Book of Revelation under the Seven Churches. The Seventh Church represented the Millennial church followed by the final judgment of the world, and then everlasting peace—remember, the Seventh Day is always represented as the Seventh Day Rest or the Sabbath Rest. This calculates from the 2,000 years of the Church (beginning B.C.E. 1 approximate date for the birth of Jesus Christ), and divide by the 6 Ages (remember the 7th is the Sabbath rest) then you will arrive at the completion of the work of the Holy Spirit in the Age of Grace—if not an exact determination of time, still a true account of the history of the Church: **"...and Jerusalem shall be trodden down of the Gentiles, until the times of the Gentiles be fulfilled"** (Luke 21:24) or another translation **"...until the appointed times of the Gentiles have expired."**

As we approach the year A.D. 2,000, it becomes even more astounding the truly inspired work written in the Book of Revelation, a Book of prophecy, authored by God, revealing the history of the Church from its infancy to its coronation. John ends Revelation 1 verse 7 with *"Even so, A'men."* This places even more emphasis on the word "Amen." It means that God said these things would happen just as they are written, and so it will be from beginning to end.

EARLY INTERPRETATION OF THE FOUR GOSPELS WITH THE SYMBOLS OF THE FOUR BEASTS OF REVELATION

The Gospel of Matthew
The symbol of the "man"

The Gospel of Mark
The symbol of the "lion"

The Gospel of Luke
The symbol of the "ox"

The Gospel of John
The symbol of the "eagle"

Ezekiel depicts the Ages of Mankind in a calendar beginning with the Time-line of Abraham; the Book of Revelation depicts the Ages of the Church beginning with birth of Jesus Christ and the Day of Pentecost.

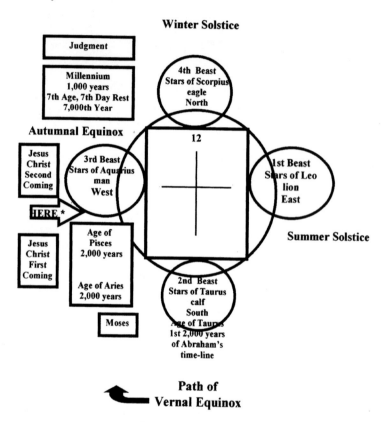

THE SEASONS OF TIME

The Vernal Equinox pinpoints the Ages from the star constellation Taurus, Aries, Pisces, to Aquarius, and in the same way Hebrew is read, moves from right to left following the PE. The Time-line of the Ages is currently (see arrow above) here (*). The "four" corners of the Earth are marked with the four main banners of the 12 Tribes of Israel as they marched through the wilderness, and named as the "four" beasts of Ezekiel and Revelation.

CHAPTER IV

THE SEVEN AGES OF THE CHURCH

The Book of Revelation addresses all Seven Churches including warnings, blessings, and the consequences of wrong actions. Each Church was faced with some form of idolatry or temptation, but only two, the Church at Smyrna and Philadelphia were spoken of most favorably.   Revelation 1:20 indicates *"...the seven candlesticks which thou sawest are the seven churches...."*

The best way to look at the time-line of the Churches in Revelation would be through Biblical references and history. The following series of examples estimates the different time-periods through the Ages of the Church and some of the events that took place during these approximate years. The last Age begins the last 2,000 years of the Church with the birth of Jesus Christ and the Church of Ephesus correlates with this time-period in history. The messages not only pertain to the Seven Churches of Asia, but also the entire Church history from Jesus Christ to Judgment.

As a further explanation, the following list of 7 Churches cover a time-span of 2,000 years divided by 6 Church Ages. The 7th Age being that of the Millennial Rest, or the Millennium. The time-periods should be considered only as an example, and the numbers are purposely rounded to the whole (note the year 666). Obviously, to recapture major events in world history would take volumes, and dates prior to A.D. 500 would need to be configured precisely, if possible.

Each of the 7 Ages of the Church are broken down and listed as follows:

(1) The "Age" from 1 to 7
(2) The title message to each Church from 1 to 7
(3) The corresponding dates in history
(4) The historical events and references associated with that particular time-period
(5) The corresponding Book of Revelation passage explaining the events in history associated with that particular time-period
(6) A brief explanation of each Church in relationship to the history associated with that time-period

---

SEVEN AGES OF THE CHURCH
FIRST AGE
(not counting zero as a year)
THE MESSAGE TO THE CHURCH AT EPHESUS
B.C.E. 1 - A.D. 332

HISTORICAL EVENTS:
From Jesus Christ to Constantine
Pentecost
Birth of Church
The Roman Empire Began in B.C.E. 27 B.C.
The Roman Empire flourished under Augustus (aka Octavian), grand nephew of Julius Caesar, the 1st Pontifex Maximus, Chief Bridgebuilder

---

*"Rev. 2:1-2: "Unto the angel of the church of Ephesus
write; These things saith he that holdeth the seven stars in
his right hand, who walketh in the midst of the seven golden
candlesticks. I know thy works, and thy labour, and thy
patience, and how thou canst not bear them which are
evil:..."*

Ephesus marks the beginning of a transition period from
the Old Testament under the law to the New Testament life in
the Spirit. This Age begins with the birth, life, death, and
resurrection of Jesus Christ, and the succession of 2,000 years
of the Church Age. It reveals the work of God as well as the
work of man, the introduction of Truth to the corruption of
falsehood.

This First Age is represented by the Church in its
infancy...its purity, as the pureness representative of the golden
candlestick, and the early Apostolic Church beginning with the
Day of Pentecost. *"Up to this time, it will be observed, the
attempts to put down the new Faith had come from the
Sadducaic party. Separated in no respect from the nation, the
members of the Christian society attended the festivals,
worshipped in the Temple and the Synagogue, and observed
the ordinances of the Law side by side with the "breaking of
the Bread" from house to house."* (8)

When John wrote Revelation, Ephesus was the capital
of Asia, and for at least two years between A.D. 55 to 57,
Ephesus became the central location of Paul's missionary
journeys and where he founded an important church. Although
the government was Roman, a mixture of Greek and Oriental
philosophies predominated the character of worship among its
inhabitants.

In Ephesus, Paul encountered the magnificent temple of
Diana (Artemis), the many-breasted, ancient, black wooden
goddess "who fell from heaven." Ancient Ephesus during the
time of Paul, existed purely as the "seat" for the use of magic,

superstition, the occult, astrology, philosophy, and thought to be the abode of every evil, foul spirit on the face of the earth.

The Ephesian people, educated and uneducated alike, harbored mysterious superstitions. The only way to dispose of evil spirits threatening harm was to recite special prayers and incantations, wear certain amulets (meaning circle, as in the heavens), symbolic necklaces, or magical symbols. *"And God wrought special miracles by the hands of Paul. So that from his body were brought unto the sick handkerchiefs or aprons, and the diseases departed from them, and the evil spirits went out of them"* (Acts 19:11-12).

—The Apostles That Are Not

Rev. 2:2: "...and thou hast tried them which say they are apostles, and are not, as hast found them liars: ...."

Here too resided the seven brothers, sons of Sceva, the Jewish High Priest, who attempted to duplicate the work of the Holy Spirit: then *"...certain vagabond Jews, exorcists..."* (Acts 19:13; perhaps early Ba'aleshem). They observed Paul casting out demon spirits. Just as Simon, the sorcerer, coveted the Holy Spirit's power for selfish gain, so did the exorcists. They noticed Paul speaking the Name of Jesus and demon spirits departed. —Most likely, they thought the Name of Jesus to be a secret name, an incantation, used for casting out demons, and *"...took upon them to call over them which had evil spirits the name of the Lord Jesus, saying, We adjure you by Jesus whom Paul preacheth"* (Acts 19:13)...to which the demon responded, *"...Jesus I know, and Paul I know; but who are ye?"* (Acts 19:15).

This response is significant as to "ownership" or possession. Paul knew the power behind the Name of Jesus, and Paul possessed the power of the Holy Spirit within him, *"...And be renewed in the spirit of your mind"* (Ephesians 4:23). The seven sons of Sceva outwardly knew the power behind the Name of Jesus, but inwardly hadn't possessed the power of the Holy Spirit: *"...according to the working of his mighty power, Which he wrought in Christ, when he raised him from the dead, and set him at his own right hand in the heavenly places, Far above all principality, and power, and might, and dominion, and every name that is named, not only in this world, but also in that which is to come"* (Ephesians 1:19-21).

Secondly, their response is significant of "authority." Because the seven sons of Sceva didn't know Jesus Christ as Lord and Savior, they had not been granted permission to speak with the power of the Holy Spirit, and therefore, had no "authority." As Paul wrote, in Jesus Christ, *"...To the intent that now unto the principalities and powers in heavenly places might be known by the church the manifold wisdom of God"* (Ephesians 3:10).

Thirdly, their response is significant of "power." Obviously, the seven sons of Sceva must have had limited success in delivering those suffering with demon possession, because this is how they built their reputation as exorcists. What they coveted was the "power" behind the speaking of the Name of Jesus, and the end result of that power when they observed Paul as he adjured evil spirits to come out: *"Finally, my brethren, be strong in the Lord, and in the power of his might. Put on the whole armour of God, that ye may be able to stand against the wiles of the devil. For we wrestle not against flesh and blood, but against principalities, against powers, against the rulers of the darkness of this world, against spiritual wickedness in high places"* (Ephesians 6:10-12).

When the evil spirit realized the seven sons of Sceva had no (1) ownership, (2) authority, or (3) power to use the Name of Jesus, it counteracted, viciously attacking them. As a result, *"...the name of the Lord Jesus was magnified"* (Acts 19:17), and many of those who practiced the occult arts (including Christians) came to believe and burned their books of magic and astrology (Acts 19:19). That is why Paul wrote to the Ephesian church, *"Wherein in time past ye walked according to the course of this world, according to the prince of the power of the air, the spirit that now worketh in the children of disobedience"* (Ephesians 2:2).

—-Emergence of False Doctrines

Rev: 2:3: "..And has borne, and hast patience, and for my name's sake hast laboured, and hast not fainted."

Then certain *"false brethren"* (Gal 2:12) began creeping into the Church with various, sundry notions and doctrines. Among some of these were converted Pharisees who went down from Judea to Antioch (Acts 15:1), and creeping in unawares began to observe how the Jewish Law was relaxed in favor of the Gentile Christians.

During the first 500 years of Christianity, every form of doctrine, philosophy, error, and untruth attempted to infiltrate Christian doctrine. We might read of many of the Christian "apologists" during this time, who wrote extensively on the "blasphemous, heretical" doctrines that soon came to be associated with Christianity.

Paul warned the church elders of Ephesus while in Miletus about what would happen after he departed for Jerusalem, *"...shall grievous wolves enter in among you, not sparing the flock. Also of your own selves shall men arise, speaking perverse things, to draw away disciples after them"* (Acts 20:28-30). Immediately, this became evident, i.e., Hymenaeus, Alexander, the coppersmith, and Philetus (I Tim. 1:20; II Tim. 2:17; 4:14-15) who began infiltrating strange doctrine into the church in an attempt to gain selfish power, and also one of the earliest known heretical teachings against the church known as Marcion's Docetism, whose members denied the physical resurrection of Jesus' body. Others, including Cerinthus, the Alexandrian Jew, "the foe of truth" (Acts 11:2;

15:1, 24; Galatians 2:4; 2 Corinthians 22:13; I John 4:2-3), denied the divinity of Jesus Christ; and included the teachings of the Ophites, Basilides, Valentinians among them.

Paul addressed one of these doctrines, known as Gnosticism, in 1 Timothy 1:4 and again, in 1 Timothy 6:20, *"Neither give heed to fables and endless genealogies, which minister questions, rather than godly edifying which is in faith....;"* and 1 Timothy 4:1-2, *"Now the Spirit speaketh expressly, that in the latter times some shall depart from the faith, giving heed to seducing spirits, and doctrines of devils. Speaking lies in hypocrisy, having their conscience seared with a hot iron...O Timothy, keep that which is committed to thy trust, avoiding profane and vain babblings, and oppositions of science falsely so called."*

HISTORICAL EVENTS:
Burning of Rome during Nero's reign A.D. 64
Persecution of Christians
Jerusalem overrun; destruction of Temple A.D. 70 by Titus, Vespasian's son
Emperor Domitian, younger brother of Titus
The Diaspora Rebellion A.D. 115-117
Jerusalem destroyed again in A.D. 131, destruction of Temple by Emperor Hadrian; Judaism forbidden
Bar-Cochebas, "the Son of Star," proclaimed himself Messiah
Jews banished from Palestine
Persecution of Christians
Martyrdom
Marcus Aurelius, Stoic philosopher whose writings paralleled Christianity
Persecution under Decius and Valerian
Goths destroy temple of Ephesus
The Septuagint found

Persian War

Worship of Magna Mater, the Oriental Great Mother, later known as Cybele; worship of Isis

Great Persecution of Christians

Diocletian - ten yrs from A.D.303 to 313 - final and worst of Christian persecutors in Roman history

Recognition of Christianity by Emperor Galerius

Edict of Milan in A.D. 313 provided tolerance for Christians

—**Leaving The First Love**

Rev. 2:4: *"...Nevertheless I have somewhat against thee, because thou hast left thy first love. Remember therefore from whence thou art fallen, and repent, and do the first works; or else I will come unto thee quickly, and will remove thy candlestick out of his place, except thou repent."*

HISTORICAL EVENTS:
Constantine Emperor from A.D. 324-337
Christianity tolerated
Council of Nicea A.D. 325
The Nicene Creed

What intermediary came between Christ and His people? At this time in history, the Christian church was pursued by many varied doctrines and beliefs. How could anyone hear the true voice of the Spirit, except they be born-again?

Constantine moved the Seat of the Roman Empire, formerly in Rome, to Constantinople, the City of Constantine (Byzantium on the Bosporus) now called the New Rome. Here he established his imperial throne, and it was from

Constantinople where the Roman Church's control and influence spread throughout the world. The once free, yet horribly persecuted Church, now found a false peace under the power of governmental rule.

Until the time of Constantine, irregardless of their persuasion—Jew, Gentile, Roman, Christian, or slave—the Christian religion was still considered a class of Judaism. The Nicene Creed basically inhibited the practice of Jewish festivals, holy days, and worship. The Jewish customs of the Christian believers were almost completely eliminated from all forms of worship. New rules and customs were instituted by the governmental church. Messianic Christianity faded into history when the decree went forth forbidding Christians from observing the Passover

The pagans began adopting the religion of the Christians and the Christians, likewise, introduced many forms of paganism into worship practices. Soon, the Messianic Christians became isolated, forbidden to worship with the Jews in synagogue (Amidah, the Eighteen Benedictions), and willingly excluded from paganized Christianity. Following the Council of Nicea, many ancient manuscripts disappeared from antiquity, were banned, or rewrote into acceptability.

—The Deeds of the Nicolaitanes

Rev. 2:4: "But this thou hast, that thou hatest the deeds of the Nicolaitanes, which I also hate. He that hath an ear, let him hear what the Spirit saith unto the churches; To him that overcometh will I give to eat of the tree of life, which is in the midst of the paradise of God."

Selfishness would be a good word classification to describe the Ephesian church of Revelation in their fallen state. Selfishness in not seeking after the truth of God's Word.

Out of all ancient of the ancient doctrines labeled "false-teaching," the pseudo-astrological cult of Mithraism would most likely be considered the closest parallel danger to Christianity.   As Rudyard Kipling wrote in, "A Song to Mithras," *"Mithra, God of the Morning, our trumpets waken the Wall! Rome is above the Nations, but Thou art over all!"* Mithraism mimicked Christian ceremony including the worship of a virgin-born savior (born on December 25th, the Winter Solstice) who died and was later resurrected.   Mithraism duplicated Christian worship practices, baptisms, and festivals with secret initiations—all, by the way, with the exclusion of women.

In the Book of Romans, Paul addresses both the Jew and Gentile, and of these, *"...who hold the truth in unrighteousness"* (Romans 1:18). Believers of whom *"...God is manifest in them..."* (Romans 1:19). But why do they "hold the truth in unrighteousness?" *"Because that, when they knew God, they glorified him not as God, neither were thankful; but became vain in their imaginations, and their foolish heart was darkened (Romans 1:21) Professing themselves to be wise, they became fools. And changed the glory of the incorruptible God into an image made like to corruptible man, and to birds, and fourfooted beasts, and creeping things"* (Romans 1:22-23).

Of the seven so-named deacons of the early church, appointed by the apostles, Nicolas, a proselyte of Antioch (Acts 6:5), was among the Hellenists chosen.   Some early scholars presumed Nicolas to be the founder of the Nicolaitans mentioned in Revelation 2:6.

The word, Nicolaitans comes from the root word, nikao, meaning "to conquer," and laos, meaning "the people." In other words, it was the act of controlling believers. Most likely, it was from another Nicholas of a later date in history, but the concept of the Nicolaitans can be found in the governmental control of the Church. And through this process, the purity of the virginal Church became corrupted by the introduction of new ideas, infiltration of pagan rites into Christian worship practices, establishment of new holy days combined with idolistic rituals, and the introduction of a new religion that would appease the fleshly desires of the majority.   With this combination, it becomes clearly evident how various superstitions were introduced into the early Church by those with fraudulent, ulterior motives of control and rule.

—*The Spirit to the Churches*

Rev. 2:7: "He that an ear, let him hear what the Spirit saith unto the churches; To him that overcometh will I give to eat of the tree of life, which is in the midst of the paradise of God."

Early Jewish sages believed The Tree of Life and the Tree of Knowledge contained the mystery of the elements of life and were forbidden knowledge (Gen 2:16-17); and because of Adam and Eve's disobedience, were forced from the Garden of Eden. The Tree of Life is the key to understanding the universe and Creation (especially used by Kabbalists). The full understanding of the elements may always remain as a mystery until revealed by God.

SECOND AGE
THE MESSAGE TO THE CHURCH AT SMYRNA
A.D. 333 - "666"

HISTORICAL EVENTS:
The Rise of the Roman Church
The Greek Mystery Religions
Rise of Oriental Religions
Julian, nephew of Constantine, the Apostate, who opposed Christianity, restored paganism and rebuilt pagan temples;

also removed laws forbidding Judaism and promised to
rebuild the Temple in Jerusalem
Christianity as State Religion under Theodosius, paganism
forbidden
Attila the Hun invades Scythia, Germany, Rome,
and Huns (Goths), Franks, Vandals, Burgundians,
Lombards, Angles, and Saxons invade Europe
Goths and Vandals sack Rome
Roman empire divided East and West; Fall of the
Western Roman Empire in A.D. 476
2nd Age brought Theodosius, Chrysostom, Ambrose,
Jerome, Augustine, Martin
Innocent I, Bishop of Rome
Leo I, Bishop of Rome, first recognized as Pope
of Rome; greatly increased papal authority
Christian era invented by Dionysius Exiguus
Calendar division: B.C.E. and A.D.
Gregory I, the Great, Bishop of Rome,
the first great Pope
Mass first taught
Increase in monastic life; vows of poverty, chastity,
and obedience
Pope, Boniface III, declared supreme over all others in
church
Separation of Greek and Roman churches
Latin as church language
Omar conquers Egypt, Syria, Palestine, Asia Minor
Mohammed A.D. 571-632; Mohammed published Koran;
Mohammed's flight from Mecca to
Medina, and later returned to capture Mecca; Baghdad
later became capital and ruled by Haroun-al-Raschid

Rev. 2:8-10: *"And unto the angel of the church in Smyrna write; These things saith the first and the last which was dead, and is alive; I know thy works, and tribulation, and poverty, (but thou art rich)...."*

Smyrna was located about 40 miles North of the city of Ephesus. Here is where Polycarp, a disciple and friend of John, came to marytrdom mixed with the shed blood of persecuted Christians that spilled over into 250 years of suffering. To those wearing the marytr's crown it was promised that none shall be **"...hurt of the second death."** From the martyr's crown to the crown of life, many were lost, but still the remnants of the Church remained strong only to face a greater threat—peace without persecution equals passivity; truth mixed with error equals false doctrines.

Emperor Justinian's edict of A.D. 543 ordered many of the ancient sacred writings destroyed; and by his decree, the practice of Judaism was strictly forbidden. The Roman Church, in an effort to abolish religious heresy, placed all Biblical interpretations and questions in the hands of the pope. The Holy Scriptures were slowly taken from the hands of the people and placed in the protection of the Church of Rome.

Dionysos was the favored deity of Smyrna. The second age of the Church brought forth the end of the first great persecutions upon believers. Diocletian's 10-year reign of terror ended with Constantine, *"...and ye shall have tribulation ten days..."* [as in a day for a year]. Constantine brought peace, generously intermixing paganism and Christianity in hopes to please all. Thus, the Christian Church became a part of the Roman state, and vice versa. Many customs, practices, and worship days remain so to this day.

"...and I know the blasphemy of them which say they are Jews, and are not, but are the synagogue of Satan. Fear none of those things which thou shalt suffer: behold, the

devil shall cast some of you into prison, that ye may be tried; and ye shall have tribulation ten days; be thou faithful unto death, and I will give thee a crown of life...He that overcometh shall not be hurt of the second death" (2:9).

During this time, a little known anti-heretical critic named Philaster of Brescia (370-390) wrote of more than 150 heresies infiltrating the Christian Church. One of these being the *"...practice of using heathen names for the days of the week...."* (9) Among Philaster's other writings included his objections over the practice of instituting prayers for the dead (an ancient Roman practice), worship of saints, and worship of the angels (a carryover from Roman idol worship).

Who is a Jew in the sense of Revelation? The Bible states, *"He is not a Jew, which is one outwardly; neither is that circumcision, which is outward in the flesh; but he is a Jew* [as in belonging to Jesus Christ], *which is one inwardly; and circumcision is that of the heart, in the spirit,and not in the letter...."* (Romans 2:28, 29; see also Romans 9:6, 7; Galatians 3:28, 29).

It was even more than this—the early Christians were Jews who practiced not only the Sabbath, but also the breaking of bread together. Even through great persecution, there remained a remnant of Messianic Christians who continued to observe the Passover, the Jewish Sabbath, and other days common to both Judaism and Christianity. Many of these early believers followed the "new moon" announcements that were dispatched by the Jews (Beit Din later known as Patriarchs) in order to observe the proper feast days. This continued well into the 4th Century until the Roman government prohibited the Jewish couriers from dispatching any further announcements. This action brought about the later development of a fixed calendar for calculating the various months, years, and dates for particular feast days.

Also, during this part of Church history, the growth of Greek mystery religions expanded still further. Paul wrote of the wine god, Dionysos, "the sin-bearer" and a god of the elements, when he wrote of the "elemental deities" in Galatians. The "elemental deities" were the gods of Fire, Air, Earth, and Water:

> *Howbeit then, when ye knew not God, ye did*
> *service unto them which by nature are no gods.*
> *But now, after that ye have known God, or*
> *rather are known of God, how turn ye again*
> *to the weak and beggarly elements, whereunto*
> *ye desire again to be in bondage? Ye observe*
> *days, and months, and times, and years* (4:8-10).

Paul told the Galatians not to *"turn ye again to the weak and beggarly elements, whereunto ye desire again to be in bondage?"* The Greek word for the elements is "stoicheia" also known as the ZODIAC signs "stoicheiomata" of astrology. Paul was speaking about the elements of nature and the elements of the universe "ta stoicheia tou kosmou." Simply, Paul speaks about the 12 astrological signs of the zodiac. When Paul referred to, *"Ye observe days, and months, and times, and years"* (Galatians 4:8-10), he was talking about following horoscope predictions.

Jesus' body was not made of the elemental composition of this world, nor was His body subject to the elements. He was immaculately conceived, not born of the earth, or of the flesh.

> *...The first man Adam was made a living soul;*
> *the last Adam was made a quickening spirit.*
> *Howbeit that was not first which is spiritual,*
> *but that which is natural; and afterward that*
> *which is spiritual. The first man is of the*
> *earth, earthy: the second man is the Lord from*
> *heaven. As is the earthy, such are they also*
> *that are earthy: and as is the heavenly, such*
> *are they also that are heavenly. And as we*
> *have borne the image of the earthy, we shall*
> *also bear the image of the heavenly.*

Ancient people worshipped the elements, but Jesus, as Lord over the entire universe, demonstrated to mankind His mastery over the elements, and this was   something reserved only for the gods. Why was Jesus Christ any different?

Jesus walked on **water** - defying the element of water; calmed the seas, changed water into wine. Only a "god" such as Dionysos could change water into wine? Now we can be baptized with water *"...unto repentance"* (Matthew 3:11). The Greeks worshipped the god, Demeter, with bread. As the "the savior and purifier of souls," the gods, Dionysos and Demeter represented the Grecian gods of the great "Mysteries" and immortality. Thus, we read in Matthew 26:26:

> *Jesus took bread, and blessed it, and brake it,*
> *and gave it to the disciples, and said,*
> *Take, eat, this is my body. And he took the cup,*
> *and gave thanks, and gave it to them, saying,*
> *Drink ye all of it; For this is my blood of the*
> *new testament, which is shed for many for the*
> *remission of sins.*

Jesus' body was made of the same physical constitution as the pre-fallen physical nature of Adam, and yet His body did not surrender to the elements when He died. His body didn't return to the **earth** "as in dust you shall return." His body didn't decay, corrupt, or destruct. Jesus defied earth's elements - the earth could not hold Him. Jesus Christ rose from the dead in body and in Spirit. *"But now is Christ risen from the dead, and become the firstfruits of them that slept"* (I Cor. 15:20). "The sting of death is sin," and Jesus had no sin. Only Jesus could overcome death and destruction. Jesus Christ has power over the earth, as He proved when He raised Lazarus from the dead, and when He healed the sick.

Jesus defied the element of **air** - gravity could not keep Him on the earth at His ascension. The Assyrian's worshipped the elemental deity of "air," symbolizing "the spirit," but Jesus Christ, as Lord over the elements, sent the Holy Spirit. Finally, Jesus sent the **fire** of the Holy Spirit at Pentecost (worshipped by the Greeks as Hephaistos), *"...and there appeared unto* *them cloven tongues like as of fire, and it sat upon each of them... "* and *"...he shall baptize you with the Holy Ghost, and with fire. "* (Acts 2:3; Matthew 3:11).

How is Jesus Christ different that the ancient gods of the elements? Jesus Christ is Lord over the elements!

THIRD AGE
THE MESSAGE TO THE CHURCH AT PERGAMOS
A.D. 667 - 1000

HISTORICAL EVENTS:
Hegira of Mohammed
Council of Whitby
Charlemagne, A.D. 768-814, declared Holy Roman Emperor (A.D. 800), King of France, Rome, Italy, and Germany
Seventh church council at Nice
Seven kings unite-form kingdom of England under Egbert
Normans plunder Paris
Nicholas I, Pope
Alfred the Great fortified England
Edward I, King of England
Russia attacks Constantinople
Otto the Great, Emperor of Rome A.D. 962
The Dark Ages of the Church
The Golden Age of the Jews

Pope Leo III crowned the German warrior named Charlemagne (a successor of Clovis) Emperor of the Romans on Christmas Day in A.D. 800. Under Charlemagne's decree of A.D. 789, all religious affiliations came under the headship of Rome.

Charlemagne established religious schools of higher learning, developed missionary conquests throughout Europe, and numerous monasteries flourished with the specific purpose of "correcting" the entire Old and New Testament Scriptures. Only the sermons issued by royal decree could be preached anywhere in the kingdom.

Rev. 2:12: *"And to the angel of the church in Pergamos write; These things saith he which hath the sharp sword with two edges; I know thy works, and where thou dwellest, even where Satan's seat is: and thou holdest fast my name, and hast not denied my faith, even in those days wherein Antipas was my faithful martyr, who was slain among you, where Satan dwelleth. But I have a few things against thee, because thou hast there them that hold the doctrine of Balaam, who taught Balac to cast a stumblingblock before the children of Israel, to eat things sacrificed unto idols, and to commit fornication. So hast thou also them that hold the doctrine of the Nicolaitanes, which thing I hate. Repent; or else I will come unto thee quickly, and will fight against them with the sword of my mouth. He that hath an ear, let him hear what the Spirit saith unto the churches; To him that overcometh will I give to eat of the hidden manna, and will give him a white stone, and in the stone a new name written, which no man knoweth saving he that receiveth it."*

Pergamos was farther North of both Ephesus and Smyrna, and known for its eloquent philosophers of science and medicine. The name Pergamos means, "elevation or height," and it was during this time-period where the Roman Church took its foremost position in the world, and thus assumed *"...the doctrine of the Nicolaitanes."*

Residing in the city of Pergamos were the most learned men of culture who frequently visited the enormous city library to study. John wrote of Pergamos as the place where "Satan dwelleth," which came in the form of ancient "sun worship," and it was *"...Balaam, who taught Balac to cast a stumblingblock before the children of Israel, to eat things sacrificed unto idols, and to commit fornication."* It was here where the "god of medicine and healing," Asclaepius was worshipped in his own magnificent temple. Luke, the physician, undoubtedly knew of Asclaepius as the counter-part for Jesus Christ when he wrote his epistle, just as Mythraism had demonstrated.

Jude, the brother of James, wrote similarly in regard to false teachers and doctrines, *"For there are certain men crept in unawares, who were before of old ordained to this condemnation, ungodly men....Woe unto them! for they have gone in the way of Cain, and ran greedily after the error of Balaam for reward, and perished in the gainsaying of Cor'e...foaming out their own shame, wandering stars, to whom is reserved the blackness of darkness for ever"* (Jude 1:4-16). Jude speaks of the rebellious, murderers, idolaters, and those diviners that practice lies (Gen. 4:1-15; Numbers 16:1-40; 22-24). The same false teachers represented in II Peter 2.

Jerome's Vulgate uses the word "augures" in the Book of Jude to interpret the word for diviners. The same word is used in Deut. 18:10-14; Jeremiah 27:9, 50:36; Jude 1:13; 1 Samuel 6:2; and Isaiah 19:3. These were the lying prophets, diviners, dreamers (Jude 1:8), soothsayers, astrologers, sorcerers, etc., who deceive people into believing and following after their ungodly principals.

FOURTH AGE
THE MESSAGE TO THE CHURCH AT THYATIRA
A.D. 1001 - 1334

HISTORICAL EVENTS:
Dark Ages of the Church Continue
The Golden Age of the Jews Continue (briefly)
Abraham ibn Ezra A.D. 1092-1167; Maimonides (1135)
Pope Gregory IX issued a decree to condemn the Talmud (1239)
Jews dispersed from England (1290); wandering and longing for a homeland

Massacre and Persecution of Jews (1298, 1336-1338)
Pope of Rome Supreme
Confusion between Empire and Papacy;
corruption of papal office
Norman conquest of England
William the Conqueror
Jerusalem taken by Turks
First, Second, Third, Fourth, Fifth, Sixth, Seventh, and
Eighth Crusades
Waldenses & Albigenses
Richard Lion Heart
Persecution of Jews
Turkish recapture Jerusalem;
end of Jerusalem kingdom
Inquisition in France
Crusade against Albigenses
Scriptures forbidden to most
Dante set the standard for Italian language
Edward II of England

Rev. 2:18-29: *"And unto the angel of the church in Thyatira write; These things saith the Son of God, who hath his eyes like unto a flame of fire, and his feet are like fine brass; I know thy works, and charity, and service, and faith, and thy patience, and thy works; and the last to be more than the first. Notwithstanding I have a few things against thee, because thou sufferest that woman Jezebel, which calleth herself a prophetess, to teach and to seduce my servants to commit fornication, and to eat things sacrificed unto idols. And I gave her space to repent of her fornication; and she repented not. Behold, I will cast her into a bed, and them that commit adultery with her into great tribulation, except they repent of their deeds. And I will kill her children with death; and all the churches shall know that I am he which searcheth the reins and hearts: and I will give unto every one of you according to your works. But unto you I say, and unto the rest in Thyatira, as many as have not this doctrine, and which have not known the depths of Satan, as they speak; I will put upon you none other burden. But that which ye have already hold fast till I come. And he that overcometh, and keepeth my works unto the end, to him will I give power over the nations: And he shall rule them with a rod of iron; as the vessels of a potter shall they be broken to shivers; even as I received of my Father: And I will give him the morning star. He that hath an ear, let him hear what the Spirit saith unto the churches."*

Thyatira   lay to the Southeast of Pergamos.   It was known for its fine linen and also for its famous cloth dyers. This time period brought the true Church into the Dark Ages overshadowed by the powers of the ancient Roman Church. This period is known as Jezebel and found elsewhere in Revelation in the symbol of *"the mother of harlots and abominations of the earth"* (Rev. 17-19), specifically directed to "false teachings and the seducing of God's servants."

The Dark Ages, so aptly named, plunged the Christian Church into years of confusion, loss of identity, infiltrated from within and without with every form of superstition and abominable error. Powerful positions within the Church could be purchased or sold with a measure of gold.   Priests and Bishops acquired great wealth, power, and influence.   Those who objected loudly, protesting the vileness of the Roman Church, were tortured on the rack, burned at the stake, hunted, and massacred in every possible attempt to eliminate them.

FIFTH AGE
THE MESSAGE TO THE CHURCH AT SARDIS
A.D. 1335 - 1668

HISTORICAL EVENTS:
Beginning of the Hundred Years War (A.D. 1346-1453)
Plague called the "Black Death" (A.D. 1348-49); blamed Jews

**The Golden Bull of Charles IV (1356) declaring authority
over the Jews**

**5th Age brought Wickcliffe, John Huss, Joan of Arc,
Gutenberg**

Beginning of Vatican Library

**Fall of the Eastern Roman Empire with its capital
Constantinople; invaded by the Turks in A.D. 1453**

Ivan I, 1st Czar

St. Peter's Rome

**Discovery of America A.D. 1492; early explorers
such as Diaz, Da Gama, Magellan, Cortez, Pizarro; etc.**

Wycliffe, Huss, Savonarola, Erasmus, Luther, Calvin

The Reformation

**Diet   at Worms outlawed Luther; in hiding Luther
translated the Bible into German**

**Loyola founded Jesuits to fight Protestantism;
Counter-Reformation begins**

**Council of Trent; a series of meetings over 18 year
span**

**resulting in the publication of the "Index" of
forbidden books especially the Bible**

**Spanish Inquisition; cruel persecution of Protestants and
Jews**

**Persecution of Waldensians; a group of Huguenots
(Calvinists) were massacred on St. Bartholomew's Day**

**Edict of Nantes; Protestantism established and
Protestants given right to worship but forced to pay tithes
to Catholic church; Religious liberty
granted to Huguenots**

Pope Sixtus

Shakespeare

**New Translation of Bible; the first printed edition of the
Bible by William Tyndale**

Jamestown, VA settled
Thirty-years war - Germany (A.D. 1618-1648)
Puritans land-Plymouth Rock
Baghdad taken by Turks
Colonies of New England unite
Cromwell
Great fire in London

Rev. 3:1-6: *"And unto the angel of the church in Sardis write; These things saith he that hath the seven Spirits of God, and the seven stars; I know thy works, that thou has a name that thou livest, and art dead. Be watchful, and strengthen the things which remain, that are ready to die; for I have not found thy works perfect before God. Remember therefore how thou hast received and heard, and hold fast, and repent. If therefore thou shall not watch, I will come on thee as a thief, and thou shalt not know what hour I will come upon thee. Thou hast a few names even in Sardis which have not defiled their garments; and they shall walk with me in white: for they are worthy. He that overcometh, the same shall be clothed in white raiment, and I will not blot out his name out of the book of life, but I will confess his name before my Father, and before his angels. He that hath an ear, let him hear what the Spirit saith unto the churches."*

The wealthy city of Sardis lay about 30 miles South of Thyatira, and 50 miles northeast of Smyrna. Sardis was home to the wealthy kings of Lydia, among them Croesus, one of the richest men who lived in this commerically fertile region. Sardis was home to a massive temple dedicated to the goddess, Cybele.

Rome's control over the Church gave way to the Reformation. As the freedom from the grasp of Roman rule led way to the new Americas, the Church began to splinter into doctrinal groups and ideologies resulting in the Church gradually lulling itself to sleep. Perhaps, this is the reason the Sardis Church came to be known as the "dead church."

SIXTH AGE
THE MESSAGE TO THE CHURCH AT PHILADELPHIA
A.D. 1669 - 2002

HISTORICAL EVENTS:

Bloodless Revolution led to English Bill of Rights and freedom of worship to all except Jews, Catholics, and Unitarians.

Wars of Louis XIV

Ivan the Terrible, 1st Czar of Russia

Wars and Rumors of Wars including King William's War, Queen Anne's War, King George's War, French and Indian War (Seven Years' War)

Witchcraft in New England

Ben Franklin, electricity

American colleges, newspapers open, steam engine, telegraph, sewing machine, gas lighting, anesthesia, seismograph, Xray, and many other new inventions and discoveries

American Revolution

Declaration of Independence A.D. 1776

Constitution adopted

First Printed English Bible

George Washington, 1st President

Beginning of the French Revolution (A.D. 1789); The Revolution of 1830; The Revolution of 1848

Napolean Bonaparte (A.D. 1768-1821)

Franco-Prussian War; Crimean War; Russo-Turkish War; Turco-Italian War; the Balkan War; Spanish-American War

Jews build temple on Zion

Jews relief pact - England
Civil War
Civil Rights Bill
Numerous Wars throughout countries of the world
including Korean, Vietnam, WW I and II
World Evangelism
The Great Depression 1929
The sleeping Church is revived in the early 1800's, with a
renewed interest in the study of Prophecy and Israel's role
in Prophecy
Israel - a nation - May 14, 1948 (5th Day of Iyar, 5708)
Autumn of 1965, a Resolution by the Catholic Church
instituted by Pope John XXIII rejecting any further hatred
or persecution of Jews
6 Day War - 1967
Close of Church Ages

Rev. 3:7-13: *"And to the angel of the church in Philadelphia write; These things saith he that is holy, he that is true, he that hath the key of David, he tht openeth, and no man shutteth; and shutteth, and no man openeth. I know thy works: behold, I have set before thee an open door, and no man can shut it: for thou has a little strength, and hast kept my word, and hast not denied my name. Behold, I will make them of the synagogue of Satan, which say they are Jews, and are not, but do lie; behold, I will make them to come and worship before thy feet, and to know that I have loved thee. Because thou hast kept the word of my patience, I also will keep thee from the hour of temptation, which shall come upon all the world, to try them that dwell upon the earth."*

The scene depicted here portrays clearly the end of the Church Ages just prior to the Great Tribulation (known as chevlai shel Mashiach, the birth pangs of Mashiach) and known in the Old Testament as the time of Jacob's trouble. Philadelphia was 25 miles South of Sardis. The name

Philadelphia means "brotherly love," and it was founded by the
King of Pergamos, Philadelphus.

The Philadelphia Church represents the Church at its
height of evangelism, claiming the entire world for Jesus Christ.
It represents the last of the Church Ages as the ingathering and
symbolized in the words, *"behold, I have set before thee an
open door, and no man can shut it."*

Interestingly, "gates and doorways" were very
important to the Roman people. This can be observed on the
front and back of Roman coins representing "Janus," (janua in
Latin) the door god, and also known as "the spirit of the
opening." The doorway or gate entrances would be opened
when the Roman legions marched in time of war, but shut when
Rome was at peace with surrounding nations. The closing of the
gates to the Temple of Janus, for instance, during the time of
Augustus heralded a time of peace for Rome.

---

*"Behold, I come quickly: hold fast, which thou hast, that no
man take thy crown. Him that overcometh will I make a
pillar in the temple of my God, and he shall go no more out:
and I will write upon him the name of my God, and the name
of the city of my God, which is new Jerusalem, which cometh
down out of heaven from my God: and I will write upon him
my new name. He that hath an ear, let him hear what the
Spirit saith unto the churches."*

The Church at Philadelphia symbolizes the open door of
Revelation 4.

SEVENTH AGE
THE MESSAGE TO THE CHURCH AT LAODICEA
A.D. 2002 ———
PROPHECY
"no man knoweth the day or the hour"
Millennial Reign of Jesus Christ
1,000 Year Sabbath Rest for the Church

The magnificent city of Laodicea lay about 40 miles East of Ephesus. Laodicea symbolizes the "judgment," not upon the righteous, but on the unrighteous. The Laodicean Church reveals a type of apostate Church, and expresses the difference between the "wheat" and the "tares." It is a choice between identifying with the world and those things of the Earth, or belonging to the heavenly home and those things not of this Earth.

Rev. 3:14-22: *"And unto the angel of the church of the Laodiceans write; These things saith the Amen, the faithful and true witness, the beginning of the creation of God; I know thy works, that thou art neither cold nor hot: I would thou were cold or hot. So then because thou art lukewarm, and neither cold nor hot, I will spue thee out of my mouth. Because thou sayest, I am rich, and increased with goods, and have need of nothing; and knowest not that thou art wretched, and miserable, and poor, and blind, and naked: I counsel thee to buy of me gold tried in the fire, that thou mayest be rich; and white raiment, that thou mayest be clothed, and that the shame of thy nakedness do not appear; and anoint thine eyes with eye salve,that thou mayest see. As many as I love, I rebuke and chasten: be zealous therefore and repent...."*

The 7th Age - Millennium
Sabbath Rest

"Behold, I stand at the door, and knock: if any man hear my voice, and open the door, I will come in to him, and will sup with him, and he with me. To him that overcometh will I grant to sit with me in my throne, even as I also overcame, and an set down with my Father in his throne. He that hath an ear, let him hear what the Spirit saith unto the churches" *(vs. 20-22).*

If any one hears His voice, as in the sound of a trumpet, and it is those who hear that open the door to let Him in.

The same trumpet in Revelation 1:10, *"...a great voice, as of a trumpet"* is also depicted in Revelation 4:1-2, *"After this I looked, and, behold a door was opened in heaven; and the first voice which I heard was as it were of a trumpet talking with me; which said, Come up hither, and I will shew thee things which must be hereafter. And immediately I was in the spirit: and, behold, a throne was set in heaven, and one sat on the throne."*

The trumpet located behind him speaking with John signifies that John is looking at something laid out before him, similar to a map, canvas, or a panoramic picture. It is indicative of prophecy of future events ["hereafter"] based upon the past ["After this..."]: *"Write the things which thou hast seen, and the things which are, and the things which shall be hereafter" (vs19).* Here we find the trumpet immediately before the list of the Seven Churches in Rev. 1:10, and immediately after in Rev. 4.

These few words in the first sentence of Revelation 4, yield an enormous amount of prophetic symbolism.   This can be evidenced in the imagery contained in the first few words, "After this" (Meta tauta in Greek), literally means "after these things." After what things? After the Revelation of the Church Ages, the next event was "behold" which signals an awesome, wondrous sight , "a door," and the door is open, not shut. Remember: the Book of Revelation was written in Greek, but John was also Jewish.

The Hebrew root, Dalet   ד

means door, pathway, enter, lifting up, elevation, and has a numerical value of 4—unless it is written large.

From the Age of Aries through the Age of Pisces equals the equivalent of 4,000 years. Dalet and the Heh are the Hebrew root letters found in the ancient word describing the star constellation of Aquarius. The stars of the constellation of Aquarius reveal the 7,000th year:

Heh   ה

m e a n s   window, revelation, pathway, word, promise, Spirit or wind. Interestingly, another place in Scripture where the Hebrew root, Dalet, can be found is in Job 38:12-13, Psalm 110, Hosea 6:1-2, and John 1:5.

Obviously, John is writing of a Revelation, when he describes here the Catching Away (aka resurrection or Rapture - natzal) of the Church. What better way to describe the rapture than to symbolically portray it in symbolism as an open door, pathway, to enter, lift up, elevate, window (as in open), revelation (as in the Book), pathway, promise, Spirit (as in Holy), or wind?

This same reference to Heh (or the Catching Away) is depicted in the Age of Noah (Gen. 6:16) in the measure of the window of the ark, which in this example equals 1,000 years [as in 1 day = 1,000 years; 1 cubit = 1,000 years). The time-line of Abraham is found in the 3 levels of the ark. The lower level (2,000 years = First Age), second level (2,000 years = Second Age), and third level (2,000 years = Third Age) of the ark totals 6,000 years (see Luke 13:25). This, too, correlates with the year of Jubilee and the days of man (120 years x 50 years = 6,000 years).

The star constellation of Aquarius and Air can also be found in the Hebrew word for air (or wind) written as RWX (or RWX ALHYMF). This word is found in Genesis 1:2 *"...the wind of God hovered over the face of the waters...."*. The wind or air of God (Holy Spirit) communicates the Will of God.

Again, the open door and the 6,000 year time-line can be seen in Ezekiel's description of the Millennial worship. *"Thus saith the Lord God; The gate of the inner court that looketh toward the east shall be shut the six [6] working days; but on the sabbath [7th day; 7,000th year] it shall be opened, and in the day of the new moon it shall be opened."* And also in the Millennial vision of the sanctuary when Ezekiel described the 2 posts (2,000 years), the door measuring 6 cubits (6,000 years), the breadth of the door 7 cubits (7,000 years) (Ezek 41:3); and the measurements of the altar: 1 cubit (1,000 years),

2 cubits (2,000 years), 4 cubits (4,000 years), and 12 cubits (12,000 years).

Balaam's Prophecy

Balaam also refers to the Second Coming, the end of time, and the prophecy of the 12 tribes of Israel with the New Jerusalem in Numbers 24:5-7: *"How goodly are thy tents, O Jacob, and thy tabernacles, O Israel...He shall pour the water out of his buckets, and his seed shall be in many waters, and his king shall be higher than Agag* [Gog; Ez. 38] *and his kingdom shall be exalted."* NOTE: Balaam refers to the blessing, a prophecy for the seed of Jacob, not a prophecy of the stars of Aquarius describing or picturing God as depicted in the Stars in the Gospel.

In the PE the stars in the constellation of Aquarius are located on the wheel of time in the West.

The Hebrew root Tzadi **צ**
means righteous, to hunt (for insights), or harvest.

This same example in comparing Hebrew root letters with the elements of time can also be found in the ancient Jewish wedding. The depiction of the PE beginning with the Spring festivals (Age of Taurus) is seen in the ancient Jewish betrothal of the bride and groom, and will culminate in the wedding as seen in the Fall festivals (Age of Aquarius) (Talmud: Mas. Shabbat 119a; Ketubot 3b, B. Kama 32b). This is even more clearly evident in the first chapters of Revelation as depicted in the description of the seven Ages of the Church.

According to the Talmud, the Messianic Kingdom begins at the festival of Rosh HaShanah (Rosh HaShanah 10b-11a), the Festival of Trumpets ("s" meaning more than one) (Leviticus 23). The Messianic Kingdom (Athid Lavo, The Coming Age) would correlate with the interpretation of the Jewish Age of 6,000 years (six days God worked, and at the end of the six days, beginning on the 7th - 7,000th year - He rested). The 7,000th year being Athid Lavo. In September 1999, the Jewish calendar will be the year 5760. We are fast approaching the end of the 6,000 years in the time-line, so where is the missing 240 years between the Jewish calendar and the Gregorian?

Part of the answer can be found in Isaiah 20:8-11. After the death of Ahaz, his son, Hezekiah, ascended to the throne. Ahaz closed the doors of the Temple, but on the very first day of his reign, Hezekiah opened the doors of the house of the Lord (II Chron.29:3). He cleansed the Temple, introduced major religious' reforms, including restoration of the Passover, and established the observance of the other feasts.

Hezekiah fell ill and prayed to God for healing. Hezekiah asked Isaiah what would be the sign of his healing, *"...and that I shall go up into the house of the Lord the third day?"* Hezekiah spoke of the "third day" in reference to the 3,000th year after the birth of Jesus Christ which is equivalent to the 7,000th year of the time-line. This is a symbolic picture of the resurrection and rapture.

The following conversation reveals the symbolic meaning of the prophecy: Isaiah said, *"...shall the shadow go forward ten degrees, or go back ten degrees?"* Hezekiah responded, *"It is nothing for the sun to go ahead 10 degrees, but let the shadow return backward 10 degrees."* The 10 degrees is another meaning for the calendar time-period. It is a picture of a day and a year.

24 hours = 1 day X 10 degrees = 240 (240 years)

A similar reference to this time-period is found in Hosea 6:2, *"After two days will he revive us: in the third day [7,000th year] he will raise us up, and we shall live in his sight...and he shall come unto us as the rain, as the latter and former rain unto the earth."* Jesus went to the wedding ceremony on the "third day." The wedding occurs on the 3rd day or the 3,000th year after the birth of Jesus Christ. The 3,000th year is the 7th day or the 7,000th year (see also Ex. 19 and Esther 5:1).

CHAPTER V

A COMPARISON OF THE JEWISH WEDDING AND THE CHURCH IN PROPHECY

One of the best ways to describe the Second Coming is in the form of the ancient Jewish Wedding. In the ancient Jewish wedding, a bride is chosen for the groom, and at that time a covenant (or legal agreement) is made (2 Cor 11:2; Eph 5:24-25). This covenant process occurs with two contracts, and a two-step process to the betrothal. The first contractual agreement (Shitre Erusin) of marriage would be mutually agreed upon first between the husband and the father of the bride, and then the groom must in return pay a very expensive price (or dowry) (1 Cor 6:20) for the promise of his bride (PENTECOST).

The bride-to-be would then drink from a cup of wine to "seal" the betrothal. At this time the husband (Messiah) and wife (the purchased possession) would be considered betrothed (legally married) except for the consummation of the marriage union. At this point, the marriage could only be dissolved through divorce.

From the time of the contractual agreement for betrothal, the bride was set apart (waiting; 1 Thess 1:10), reserved and consecrated (1 Peter 2:9) to her husband alone. The ancient Jewish wedding mostly occurred sometime between dusk and midnight. The bride anxiously awaited, her lamps filled with oil in preparation and ready for her groom's (any moment) return (Matthew 25:6-10; 1 Cor 15:52). Her wedding attendants' waited also, with their lamps burning, in hopeful expectation of his soon return (Matthew 22:2-4; 25:3,4; Hebrews 9:28; II Peter 3:10). All of the virgins (virgins because the marriage union has not been consummated) await together in "one place" because they want to be ready so all may go together to the wedding. This ancient Jewish custom following tradition was accompanied by the "shout" and "sounding of the Shofar." The sounding of the Shofar alerted the virgins that the bridegroom was on his way to gather them for the marriage celebration.

The Kingdom of Heaven is best described by the parable of the ten virgins in Matthew 25:1-13. Here again, they are called virgins because they are not yet brides. The first paragraph of this passage begins with, ***"Then shall the kingdom of heaven be likened unto...."*** From this first sentence, it may be determined that the kingdom of heaven is a parable, and the parable associates the Jewish wedding ceremony with that of the groom "coming" for His bride.

The King who made the marriage-feast is our heavenly Father, the Bridegroom is His Son, our Lord Jesus Christ, the Bride, all those who have been purchased with a price. The wedding would be an appointed season designated sometime in the future, but with no particular day or time announced beforehand. The future time-period was not indicated precisely because the groom must go and prepare a place for "His" bride. After the groom has prepared a dwelling place for his bride, the Father then gives the groom permission to go gather his Bride to bring her to their new home.

The evening marriage ceremony symbolizes all who come from outer darkness into the light. The "oil," laid up in the vessel, represents the expression of "faith" demonstrated from an inward, spiritual supply. The "lamp" is the outward expression of "faith" demonstrated by "works." The light from the lamp is fed directly through the the supply of oil. It is the fullest expression of the Word of God revealed through His followers, as in, *"The word is a lamp unto my feet, and a light unto my path"* (Ps. 119:105; see also Prov. 6:22-23).

The ten bridesmaids are a part of the bridal party who took their lamps and went to meet the bridegroom, but not knowing when he would return, only five of them were wise enough to fill their lamps with oil. The other five were foolish and did not prepare ahead of time. They waited and waited.... The bridegroom delayed his coming (Christ's return), and so the virgins slumbered and slept (grew tired of waiting) until midnight (the appointed hour), when they were roused by the shout (a sudden cry from the two witnesses), *"The bridegroom is coming! Come out and welcome him!"*

At this point came the distinguishing mark between the two groups. All the virgins immediately jumped up and trimmed their lamps. The five who hadn't acquired enough oil noticed their lamps were "gone out," and asked the others for oil, but the wise virgins said, and notice this, *"...Not so; lest there be not enough for us and you...."* The wise virgins came prepared for the groom, while the foolish virgins did not. The bridegroom came, and those who were ready went in with him to the marriage feast, after which the door was locked.

Later, the foolish virgins returned with oil, but they remained outside shouting to open the door! The foolish virgins now realized the consequences of unpreparedness. They stood so close, but nevertheless, remained on the other side. The groom called back, *"I know you not. Watch therefore, for ye know neither the day nor the hour wherein the Son of man cometh."* The foolish virgins are the ones who never really knew the groom, Jesus Christ. They were simply empty lamp vessels who never contained the oil of the Holy Spirit.

The Jewish wedding can also be seen in God's eternal Covenant promise with Abraham. First, the Covenant is drawn with Abraham (Taurus; ALEPH), but Israel commits adultery (idolatry). Only the husband can free his wife from the bounds of marriage, and Israel's adultery forces the husbandman to dissolve the marriage bonds through divorce; but God loves

Israel with a Covenant Promise of everlasting love. He will not always forsake her, and Israel repents. Another promise is made 4,000 years later with the promised coming of the Messiah (Pisces; PENTECOST) and His death and resurrection—this is the first contractual agreement for the betrothal (Kedushin) (1 Cor 6:20; 1 Cor 7:23).

In this symbolic picture, the groom, the Messiah, is absent because he goes to *"prepare a place for her"* (John 14:2-3), his bride (the purchased possession) in his Father's chamber (chadar or chupah) for 3 days (Age of Pisces) (these are the 3 Ages of Time x 2,000 per Age = 6,000 years). This is also symbolic of Jesus' resurrection on the 3rd day, and similarly depicts the bodily resurrection of all those who have died before in Christ combined with the catching away (rapture) of those alive in Christ. Another way to view this would be from the stars in the constellations of Taurus [2,000 years]; Aries [2,000 years]; Pisces [2,000 years] = 6,000 years divided by 3 days = 2 or 2,000 years; and 2,000 years divided by 3 = 666 (in context of the 6 Ages of the Church).

If the groom is asked when the wedding will be, he replies, *"No man knows the day or the hour except my Father,"* (Mark 13:32). This is because the father must know that all of the "preparations" for the wedding ceremony have been completed (Num 28:26; Heb 10:36-37), and only then, does the groom have permission to go to his bride (1 Thess 5:2); but there is still another correlation.

Traditionally the Jewish festival of Rosh HaShanah, known as The Feast of Trumpets, always begins on a new moon, and the new moon always began each consecutive month. No one knew the exact day or hour (see Matthew 24) of the commencement of the Feast of Trumpets because it correlated with the sighting of the new moon and had to be verified by "two witnesses" (Rev. 11) who would actually "witness" the crescent of the moon before making the announcement. All of the people anxiously awaited to receive the testimony of two reliable witnesses, because only they could sanctify the New Moon. In understanding the Jewish festival of Rosh HaShanah it becomes clearer the meaning of Matthew 24:36 and Revelation 11, in that, *"No one knows about that day or hour, not even the angels in heaven, nor the Son, but only the Father."*

The Feast of Trumpets, Rosh HaShanah, is the First of the Jewish Fall Festivals and the fulfillment of Messianic prophecy. Rosh HaShanah introduces the Day of the Lord (Isaiah 26:1-3; 57:1-2) which according to the Talmud is also the resurrection of the righteous dead and catching away of believers (saints aka Tzadikim) (see Psalm 27;5; Isaiah 26:19-21, 1 Thess. 4:13-5:3). The Shofar will blow at the end of the 6,000 years of age introducing the beginning of Rosh HaShanah. Remember, Rosh HaShanah is the 1st day of the Jewish New Year. The 1st day of the 7th month (or 7,000th year). The 7th day of Creation, or 7,000th year, is the day of rest, or the Sabbath, which begins a time of peace, protection, and rest for the believer.

The days between Rosh HaShanah and Yom Kippur, the "Day of Atonement" (Yom Kippur; meaning redemption), reveal the 7-year period of Jacob's trouble or the tribulation (Joel 2:15; the 10th day of the 7th month of Tishri (Leviticus 23:32; a Day of complete Sabbath Rest). This is the Holiest Day of the Jewish Year represented in Revelation by the Second Coming, and followed by the Day of Judgment. All of those martyred throughout the tribulation will reign with the Messiah during the Sabbath "rest," the 1,000 years of the Millennium and reside in the New Jerusalem (Isaiah 11:1-12, 32:15-20; 63:1-6, Zechariah 14:1-9; Rev. 20:4-6).   When God "tabernacles or dwells," with His people in the New Jerusalem, it is symbolized with the Feast of Tabernacles.

As in the wedding ceremony, the "first" trumpet blast of the shofar announces the betrothal of the bride and groom and the last trumpet announces the wedding (Psalm 45) or "marriage supper." The final or Last Trump, final or Great Shofar (Shofar haGadol) is blown before the gates close (Matthew 25:10; Isaiah 26:20-21). Upon the closing of the gates, no others may enter

(Yom Kippur; see Isaiah 4:2-6; 27:12-13; Matthew 24:29-31; Isaiah 18:3; Joel 2:15, 17, 23). (10)

Remember: Only God knowing the "time" will open the door of the gates, and no one may enter the gates of the city until they are opened, and no one may enter after they are closed. This coincides with what Ezekiel writes in reference to the Eastern gate of the city and again in Revelation 21:25 where nothing that defiles may enter. It is at this time, after the 1,000 years, Satan will rebel with those who survived the tribulation but rejected the Messiah (Rev. 20:7-15), and be cast into the lake of fire for eternity.

This example can be further evidenced in the Jewish Civil and Religious calendar systems. Jewish festivals are determined by the Religious Calendar (Ex 12:1-2) in the Spring (Vernal Equinox, changed to Aviv following the Precession of the Equinox from Taurus to Aries) and six months later the Civil Calendar begins in the Autumn (Autumnal Equinox, Tishri), and this will mark the end of the Age in the star constellation of Aquarius.

Again, in following the wedding ceremony (Ketubah), the second contract, occurs on the 7th day after 6,000 years (DALET; during the Age of Aquarius; Hosea 2:16-20) = 6 days before the feast (Judges 14:10-18)—the bride and groom are ceremonially consecrated (Kedushin) as "pure" and stand clean, without spot or blemish (Lev 22:32-33; Isaiah 61:10). Here, in in relationship to the marriage ceremony, a portion of Hosea 2:16-20 is worth quoting in regard to Israel: *"In that day," declares the Lord, "you will call me 'my husband;'...I will betroth you to me forever...and you will acknowledge the Lord."*

The Kedushin follows another aspect of the early Jewish marriage ceremony in its connection to the prophetic time-line of 7,000 years. Traditional Jewish married couples abstained from marital relations during the 12 days following the onslaught of the monthly menses or "7 days" (7,000 yrs) after its cessation. During this time, the woman was considered separated or "unclean." At the end of her time, the wife ceremonially immersed her body in a pool of water known as "mikva." The water symbolically portraying, both physically and spiritually, the act of cleansing, and in the same association as Kedushin, the woman now stands symbolically as pure, clean, without spot or blemish (Lev 22:32-33; Isaiah 61:10), and ready to receive her husband.

Following the wedding ceremony, the bride and her groom go into the "chadar or chupah" (meaning chamber), where the groom gives gifts to his bride (Gen 24:53; Ex. 19:17; Malachi 3:16, 17), and they spend 7 days there while the wedding guests wait outside for the announcement of the marriage consummation (nesu'in) by the friends of the groom - the two witnesses (John 3:29; Rev. 11). After the announcement of the consummation, the marriage feast occurs in another celebration, and this is the Wedding Supper of the Lamb (Hosea 2:16-20; Joel 2:15; Gen 29:18-22; Esther 1-5). At the end of the week, the bride and groom go to the house prepared for them (Revelation 19:7; 21:9,10). NOTE: Luke 12:36 states when Jesus Christ returns, He will be returning from a wedding. Also notice the virgins "go forth" as the bride to meet the bridegroom, while the guests are not presented as a bride to the bridegroom.

The "chadar or chupah" is very important because that is where the husband of the bride is preparing a place for her in His chamber, and even though it is written in Greek, the entrance to the chupah is described in Hebrew by the "open door" of heaven in the Book of Revelation (4:1). The open door is the entrance way to the chamber prepared for the Church. It is the Throne Room of the Messiah; and notice, the wedding guests are waiting and watching.

Now look at the Revelation depicted in the 6th Age of the Church represented by the Message to the Church at Philadelphia:

"...he that openeth, and no man shutteth; and shutteth, and no man openeth; I know thy works: behold, I have set before

thee an open door, and no man can shut it:...I also, will keep thee from the hour of temptation, which shall come upon all the world, to try them that dwell upon the earth...Him that overcometh will I make a pillar in the temple of my God, and he shall go no more out; and I will write upon him the name of my God, and the name of Jerusalem, which cometh down out of heaven from my God..." (Rev. 3:7-13).

The last Age of the Church is depicted in the Jewish interpretation of "Athid Lavo"—The end of the Church Age and the beginning of the Millennium known as, "The Coming Age."

The Miracle in Cana

This wedding ceremony is also evident in John 2 and explained further in John 3, with the marriage feast in Cana of Galilee when Jesus turned water into wine. *"And both Jesus was called, and his disciples, to the marriage. And when they wanted wine, the mother of Jesus saith unto him, They have no wine. Jesus saith unto her, 'Woman, what have I to do with thee? mine hour is not yet come.' His mother saith unto the servants, Whatsoever he saith unto you, do it. And there were set there six waterpots of stone...the governor of the feast called the bridegroom, And saith unto him, Every man at the beginning doth set forth good wine; and when men have well drunk, then that which is worse: but thou hast kept the good wine until now."*

This miracle performed by Jesus Christ reveals the prophecy of the end of time with the revelation of the promised redemption and the remnant seed, *"Thus saith the Lord, As the new wine is found in the cluster, and one saith, Destroy it not; for a blessing is in it: so will I do for my servants sakes, that I may not destroy them all. And I will bring forth a seed out of Jacob, and out of Judah an inheritor of my mountains: and mine elect shall inherit it, and my servants shall dwell there"* (Isaiah 65:8-9).

In the Jewish calendar we are soon to enter a different age. A time-period marked in the heavenly calendar by the stars of the constellation of Aquarius. The Hebrew letter, Daleth, is found in the root word for the Hebrew name of the constellation of Aquarius, and Daleth means "door," or path, entrance way, etc. Rosh HaShanah is also known as YomhaDin, the Day of Judgment, where one's name is either written, or not written, in the Book of Life. The awakening blast of the Shofar just before Rosh HaShanah, is a time for the repentance of sins, a day of remembrance (Lev. 23, Ez. 33:1-7, Malachi 3:16, II Cor).

The wedding ceremony, the Jewish feasts, and return of the Lord can best be summarized in the beautiful passaged contained in James 5:7-9: *"Be patient therefore, brethren, unto the coming of the Lord. Behold, the husbandman waiteth for the precious fruit of the earth, and hath long patience for it, until he receive the early and latter rain. Be ye also patient; stablish your hearts: for the coming of the Lord draweth nigh. Grudge not one against another, brethren, lest ye be condemned: behold, the judge standeth before the door."*

CHAPTER VI

THE THRONE-ROOM OF THE MESSIAH

"After this I looked, and, behold, a door was opened in heaven: and the first voice which I heard was as it were of a trumpet..."(vs. 1).   John saw a door opened (as in the entrance to heaven) to receive those who are invited to enter. The heavens represent God's domain, His Throne-Room.   John wrote, "immediately," he was in the spirit, and what a perfect way to describe the catching away of believers in Jesus Christ: *"In a moment, in the twinkling of an eye, at the last trump; for the trumpet shall sound, and the dead shall be raised incorruptible, and we shall be changed"* (I Cor 15:52).

The last trumpet clearly identifies with the Jewish festival of Rosh HaShanah (the Feast of Trumpets), and remember, Rosh HaShanah also means the "opening of the gates of heaven," depicting the resurrection (7th month; 7,000th year; the Millennial or Sabbath Rest; on the star calendar at the Vernal Equinox of Aquarius).   The "opening of the gates of heaven" is also symbolized by the "open door" in Revelation 4:1.

When John witnessed the Throne-Room in heaven he saw the One sitting on the Throne and He was God (vs. 2). How can anyone comprehend the magnificence of God?   The best way to describe Him in words is as a King, and King's reside on Thrones, and His Throne sits in the center of His Kingdom -

heaven. What do we see when looking up into heaven? Of course, stars, planets, light, and what better way to describe heaven than in the precious stones of the Kingdom. Who is the foundation? One who appears as jasper and a sardine stone surrounded by a rainbow described in terms of precious gem stones (Rev. 4:3 and 21:19). The same precious gems consistent in the New Jerusalem, the Throne-Room of God on Earth, and it is He who *"...layeth the foundation of the earth..."* (Zech. 12:1).

Revelation 4:4 may be a little difficult to understand, unless you view the heavens and time as John wrote them in context and symbolism with the entire Book of Revelation. In this respect, God is in control of "time," and the Book of Revelation reveals God's timetable as depicted in the following verse:

"And round about the throne [in heaven (see vs. 2); the sun is the center of our universe just as the Son of God is on the throne in the middle of His kingdom] *were four and twenty seats* [24 divisions of one day]*: and upon the seats I saw four and twenty elders sitting* [24 hours = 1 day; the hours "lead" or guide the day], *clothed in white raiment* [a symbolism for undefilement; purity before corruption]*; and they had on their heads crowns* [another symbol for rulership; victory over sin and death] *of gold* [a final reward]*"* (Rev. 4:4).

There are 24 hours in one day, and who are "elders" other than the leaders and overseers of a church? A 24-hour time-period oversees 1 day. The Word "elders" (Greek word presbuteros) is referenced at least 12 times in the Book of Revelation. The 24 elders are representative of those who have received crowns (vs 10) of marytrdom during the persecutions of the first 6 Ages of the Church (24 x 6 = 144). They were among those who were given, *"...white robes..."* that *"...they should rest yet for a little season, until their fellow servants also and their brethren, that should be killed as they were, should be fulfilled"* (6:11).

To make things more interesting, if the 24 elders are divided by the 6 Ages of the Church the total equals the equivalent of the 4 Beasts of Revelation (4:6). The 4 Beasts are represented in the chart on Page 52. The planets and stars are described as the *"seven lamps of fire burning"* (see Zechariah 3:9; 4:10, and Ez. 1:13), and the *"sea of glass like unto crystal"* is obviously the firmament of heaven. The sun, moon, and five known planets consist of the "seven lamps of fire burning" amidst the firmament (sea of glass) of heaven. The planets and the firmament stand "before the throne" (vs. 5-6). The Kingdom of Heaven and God's Throne Room   exists beyond our known solar system.

"And out of the throne proceeded lightnings and thunderings and voices...(4:5). Here Revelation coincides with The Book of Ezekiel, *"And the living creatures ran and returned as the appearance of a flash of lightning"* (Ez. 1:14). In the same way as John, Ezekiel wrote, *"...the heavens were opened, and I saw visions of God"* (1:1).

"And the first beast was like a lion, and the second beast like a calf, and the third beast had a face as a man, and the fourth beast was like a flying eagle" (vs. 7).

The word translated "beast" in the verses 6-8 comes from the Greek word, "zoa," meaning "living ones" which are different than the beast [therion] (the anti-christ) for instance, used in Chapter 13.

In Ezekiel 1:10, a description can be found of the same four symbols as in Revelation 4:6: *"As for the likeness of their faces, they four had the face of a man* [stars of Aquarius], *and the face of a lion* [stars of Leo], *on the right side, and they four had the face of an ox* [stars of Taurus] *on the left side, they four also had the face of an eagle* [stars of Scorpius]."

The man, lion, ox, and eagle reveal time-periods, and match precisely with the time-periods following the time-line of the Vernal Equinox (see Page 52), the 24 elders, and the 4 beasts of Revelation. Ezekiel used the term "they four" in each sequence of four beasts because the four descriptions depicted four separate divisions in the entirety of time—they were separate but one unit.

Again, look at Page 52, if you look at the face of circle with picture of the Beast placed appropriately, it would be obvious that the lion is on the "right side" (East) opposite the man (West), and since the Vernal Equinox moves from right to left, the left of the lion would be the ox (or bull; South) opposite the eagle (North). Revelation 4:6 refers to these four solstice and equinox points: Leo (East-lion), the lion of Judah is on the East coinciding with the Summer Solstice, Aquarius (West-man) is on the opposite side in the West, Autumnal Equinox, the calf (South-calf) associates to Taurus, and the flying eagle (North) coincides with Scorpius.

The description in Ezekiel matches the four cardinal signs of the solstices and equinoxes, and the ensigns of the four leading divisions of the tribes of Israel (Numbers 2; Judah, Reuben, Ephraim, and Dan; see Ch. VII). Some scholars believe these to be cherubic faces (Ez. 10:20), or forms (che, as like; rab, he was great), because the ancient Jewish people believed that the cherubim represented the "holy of holies" when YHWH came to Israel at Mt. Sinai. These same cherubic faces had been presumed to be in Solomon's temple, and also the same cherub to stand guard at the Gates of Eden.

> *From the guardian Cherubim*
> *Framed appear these signs, by him*
> *Who those mystic forms had seen;*
> *Faces four, where placed between*
> *The Lion, who the prey will rend,*
> *And Bull in sacrifice to bend,*
> *The second Adam, to be slain,*
> *But eagle-like come down again.*

In their names that tongue divine
We trace, as in the patriarch line.... (11)

Some early Christian scholars associated the four cherubic faces with the bull (God, the Father), the lion (Jesus, the Son), the man (the sacrificed Son), and the eagle (the Holy Spirit); but there is no scriptural foundation for this premise. This was probably assumed as such because they didn't understand the meaning of the time-period represented by the Beast.

Ezekiel's description of the Beasts is similar to the Babylonian's conception of the universe in that the heavens consisted of a constantly moving, swirling dome-shaped sky filled with a splattering of stars and a vast sea of water. To the Babylonians, the heavens were where the gods of creation resided; but to the Jews, the heavens were the throne-room of God, and they renamed this expansive dome, "the firmament" (rakeea; see Ez. 1:22); in other words, "outer space."

As viewed from the Earth, the early (Ptolemaic) theory of the universe appeared to make sense. To the ancient observers, the sun, moon, and the planets all revolved around the Earth in apparent smaller circles (epicycles) within greater circles as in Ezekiel: *"...and their work was as it were a wheel in the middle of a wheel"* (Ezekiel 1:16). As a student of Plato, Heraclides (300 B.C.), describes these epicycles as "loops."

"Also out of the midst thereof came the likeness of four living creatures" (Ezekiel 1:4). Ezekiel describes their "likeness" and further explains their "appearance." Ezekiel was describing something in the heavens that appeared to have "life" because they moved. The ancient people thought the stars and planets to be angels, cherubim, and actual living creatures who occasionally stopped in their course before resuming.

Ezekiel's vision was a more realistic view of the universe, and similar to a Platonic viewpoint. He writes of *"the likeness of the firmament"* (1:22-23). The first chapter of Ezekiel compares the symbolism with that of the "likeness" or "appearance" of the Lord (see Rev. 4:3-5).

Ezekiel is aware that clouds bring rain (1:28), and he describes the heavens, the stars and planets as they, *"...were joined one to another; they turned not when they went; they went every one straight forward"* (vs. 9). When we look upward into the heavens it would be hard to miss the twinkling lights that brighten the night sky, *"...As for the likeness of the living creatures; their appearance was like burning coals of fire, and like the appearance of lamps"* (vs. 13; Rev. 4:5). Ezekiel then continues to describe the heavens as "a wheel" along with its colors, appearance, movement (vs. 14-25), *"and the fire was bright, and out of the fire went forth lightning"* (1:13).

Many people think that stars are colorless or simply a glittering silvery-white color, but this isn't true. The stars and planets have color determined largely by their temperature spectrum; and the color of stars can change as to whether they move toward the earth or away from the earth. Stars are measured in their degree of brightness which is called "magnitude." Stars can be blueish hot (as the deep, brilliant blue of the sapphire, Ezek. 2:26), deep green as an emerald, orange-yellow, poppy-red, or clear as jasper (Ezek. 1:16,26-28).

For instance, among the four beasts described in Ezekiel and Revelation are four stars of the first magnitude which can be seen without the aid of a telescope: Regulus (Alpha Leonis) in Leo (actually a double star) is a white star and its smaller companion a deep, dusky blue; Fomalhaut (Alpha Piscis Austrini; Hebrew, Dagim), the Southern Fish, is in Pisces Austranus/Aquarius, a sea-farer's navigational star, a reddish, solitary star.   Also, the bright reddish/orange star Aldebaran (Alpha Tauri) is in Taurus, and Antares (Alpha Scorpii), a giant, poppy-red star with its emerald green companion, is known as "the rival of Mars" and is found in Scorpius.

Ezekiel described the color of stars when he wrote "beryl, crystal, sapphire, and amber" (1:16-27); and these colors describe the "Four Royal Stars" (the beasts) of Revelation with their smaller clusters or companion stars. And, as in Revelation,

Ezekiel arrives at the conclusion as to "Who" sits over and above all of the living creatures, the stars and planets: *"And above the firmament that was over their heads was the likeness of a throne...and upon the likeness of the throne was the likeness as the appearance of a man above upon it"* (Ch. 26; Rev. 4). If the firmament represents the sky, then above the firmament is the "throne of God." Ezekiel describes the King of Glory, the Creator by whom all things were made, *"...This was the appearance of the likeness of the glory of the Lord"* (vs. 28). (See also Ezekiel 10:14, 11:20; Revelation 4:7-8).

Nature reflects God's Creation, and Creation reflects God's Glory, *"Holy, holy, holy, Lord God Almighty, which was, and is, and is to come"* (Rev. 4:8). The stars in their "appearance" and "likeness" (Ezek. 1:5,10,13,14,16,22,26,27), reflect in the association with words that which cannot be verbally expressed in describing the greatness and glory of God.

The 4 beasts of Revelation and 6 wings about "him" can be seen reflected in a depiction of the wheel of wheels of time. How would wheels move except they had "wings?" The four beasts round about the throne *"...full of eyes before and behind...and were full of eyes within"* (Rev. 4:6 and 8), reveal the periods of "time," both past, present, and future. Remember as written earlier, God is in control of "time." There are 24 hours in one day, and who are "elders" other than the leaders and overseers of a church? These 24 are representative of those who have received crowns of marytrdom during the first 6 Ages of the Church persecutions (24 elders divided by 6 Ages = 4 beasts; and 6 x 24 = 144). All of these things are reflected in verse 11: *"Thou art worthy, O Lord, to receive glory and honour and power: for thou hast created all things, and for thy pleasure they are and were created."*

CHAPTER VII

THE FOUR HORSEMEN

Rev. 5:1: "And I saw in the right hand of him that sat on the throne a book written within and on the backside, sealed with seven seals"

The Chapters between Revelation 5 and 12, have been a great puzzle to the earliest of scholars, such as Dupuis, who found them to be a "confusing enigma," and who could "give no further explanation," as to their meaning. Among the greatest mysteries of Revelation 5, is the identity of the Four Horsemen, and the meaning of the book with "7" seals. This book held a great message, because it could only be opened by the "one who is worthy," and only the one who is worthy could "loose" whatever "prophecy" is contained in the seals.

Revelation (vs. 3) reveals that no man in heaven or in earth could open the book except One, the Lion of Judah, *"hath prevailed,"* the Root of David, Jesus Christ, the *"Lamb as it had been slain"* (vs.5-9).   The only way to open the Book was through the Death and Resurrection of the Sacrificed Lamb (vs. 6).   The book or "scroll" is a period of prophetic time and held in the hand of God until "the time period" has been fulfilled, and for this reason, the beasts and elders (representing time periods) *"fell down before the Lamb"* (vs. 8)—for the time has come.

These were the "redeemed" (vs. 9) of the Earth *"...ten thousand times ten thousand, and thousands of thousands"* (vs. 11; see Deut. 33:13-17). They represent the redeemed of the 6,000 years in the time-period located on the celestial calendar at the Vernal Equinox of Aquarius/Capricornus. These star constellations are considered as Ephraim/Manasseh and joined together under Joseph, and redeemed *"...by thy blood out of every kindred, and, tongue, and people, and nation"* (vs. 9).

Rev. 6:1: "And I saw when the Lamb opened one of the seals, and I heard, as it were the noise of thunder one of the four beasts [depicting time] ***saying, Come and see*** [prophecy]*"***

As indicated in previous chapters, the Book of Revelation reveals time-periods that indicate past, present, and future revelations of prophecy. The four horsemen of Revelation 6, reveal this time-period marked by the stars of Aquarius, Capricornus, Sagittarius, and Scorpius (see pg. 44 & 118). They represent 1/4 of the 360 degree end-date calendar.

Many early scholars represent this first chapter of Revelation 6, as that of Jesus Christ because of the symbols of power depicted in the verses; but on the contrary, Verse 1 reveals the opposite of the rider in Revelation 19:11 (see also Psalm 45). The first seal brings forth the revelation of the emergence of the anti-christ and the Great Tribulation—it is the opening of the seals of prophecy.

First, it is important to remember the symbol for the four beasts is in the representation of a giant time-piece recording the span of heaven and earth from beginning to end. The time-period between the third beast man, Aquarius, and the fourth, the flying eagle, Scorpius, reveals the last years of time beginning with the opening of the Seven Seals. These periods of time depict a week of 7 days equaling 7 years (a day for a year). The book of Daniel (9:26-27; 11:19-22) gives us a closer depiction of this 7 year period and Revelation 6:2 gives the clearer picture of the one who rules during this 7 year period.

The Seals of Revelation could only portray the Great Tribulation. The 1st through the 4th of the seals represent living beings including horses through a period of tribulation, but the 5th through the 7th of the seals reveal God's judgment, wrath, those martyred during the time of great tribulation and their salvation pictured standing before the Throne of God.

The White Horse

For several years prior to A.D. 2000, many people have sounded the alarm in preparation for possible Y2K computer shutdowns and the resulting problems from world wide chaos. Actually, this forewarning isn't necessarily the ticking down of the Y2K clock, but the approaching sound, the pounding hoofbeat of THE RIDER ON THE WHITE HORSE.

"And I saw, and behold a white horse: and he that sat on him had a bow; and a crown was given unto him: and he went forth conquering, and to conquer" (Rev. 6:2).

Here Revelation describes "times" and "persons" using the stars and constellations in reference to the "bow," "crown," the "white horse," etc. All of these symbols depict a "man" with the power to subdue, conquer, and rule.

Some scholars such as Rolleston in "Mazzaroth" (1862), feel this passage to be a reference to Jesus Christ, but remember, the Messiah isn't represented symbolically as one of the seals, but it was He who "loosed and opened the seven seals" (see Rev. 19:11); nor is He depicted as a conqueror here but Jesus Christ is symbolized as a "Lamb." The sacrificial Lamb in Rev. 6 returns as the conquering King in Rev. 19:11. Here in Rev 6:2, Jesus Christ "loosed" the seals. What was once held back, has been released and loosed upon heaven and earth. The one released is the coming anti-christ (anti means opposite) or "the one who opposes Christ."

It was one of the beasts who said, "come and see." The beasts are representative of Time. The "Time" is at hand! Bau [Egyptian] is the verb "to come," and the noun derived from it, in the hieroglyphic, as in the Hebrew [bo or boh] and Greek [baion, as in branch], but also, according to Rolleston, is a "beast," "...hence a beast or beast's head is a hieroglyphic sign for "who comes." The rider on the horse "who comes" is the anti-christ who clearly goes forth to conquer the world subduing through power without defeat. This power could only be accomplished through permission, and only the Lamb could open the seals (Matt. 28:18).

Within the constellations, what star patterns symbolically portray a "bow" or "white horse?" Counting in star constellation-time periods, Sagittarius appears above the third beast, the man of Aquarius (Aquarius includes Capricornus) after the 6,000th year. The Latin name of Sagittarius depicts the archer, going forth, as in the Hebrew Kesith, and in the Arabic as Al Kaus, meaning the arrow. Another Arabic name for Sagittarius is Ruchba er rami, or "the riding of the bowman," and the Chinese render this constellation as Gjin Ma, "man-horse." Sagittarius came to be known as Centaurus (the Despised) and the Centaur (later to be known as Sagittarius the archer and first associated with Nergal's arrow shooting god of war).

The chief star in this decan is CHEIRON (the pierced, who later came to be known as Zeus) a Greek word which means means the pierced and symbolized as 1/2 man and 1/2 horse. Ancient legend portrays Cheiron as the one who fathered the constellations and who taught early man how to read the sky. The "crown" worn by Cheiron is called, Corona Australis the "Southern" crown. The meaning is symbolic of the archer who sends forth an arrow; but in Rev. 6:2, the rider only carries a bow, without mention of an arrow (see Zech. 9:14).

Here it is obvious the conqueror initially comes through peace. He is also "given" a crown before a victory where he has not earned it; therefore, it is not a victorious crown but one that nevetheless still denotes royalty and imperial power. The crown is symbolized in the crown identified with the white crowned horses of the Centaurs (the Gandharvas, or Sirens). Some early scholars have associated Sagittarius with the white horse named Pegasus, the winged-horse in Aquarius, who goes forth with the crowned rider, conquering and to conquer. Pegasus was a horse belonging to the gods, and ridden by none other than "a son of a god, Nimrod."

In the Persian zodiac Sagittarius is shown as a man with a crooked beak on his head [depicted as a horn and later as a "crown"], like the Assyrian eagle-god, Nisroch. The supreme deity of the Semitic people of Assyria was Asshur, the son of Shem, worshipped under the name of "Nisroch." The Persian Zoroaster indicated that "God has the head of a hawk," giving further evidence to the eagle-headed, Nisroch, pictured so frequently in Assyrian relics. In fact, the ancient name for Assyria was most likely Asshur. Asshur, symbolized by the "winged sun-disk," was called "the great Lord," "the King of all the Gods," and "he who rules supreme over the gods."

REPRESENTATIONS OF A WINGED DEITY, SUPPOSED TO BE THE GOD ASSHUR, THE SUPREME PATRIARCH OF ASSYRIA. (from Layard)

Both Asshur and Marduk (as Nimrod) were worshipped as gods, mostly because of their prowess for conquering nations [the horn, crown, symbolic of power] and thereby acquiring great wealth. A good example of this power is found in Hosea 14:3, *"Asshur shall not save us, we will not ride upon horses...Ye are our gods...."*

The entrances to Assyrian temples contained images of grotesque figures of "winged bulls," "lions with human heads," or "lions with hawk heads." These same symbols could be found marked on Babylonian or Assyrian military standards. The eagle (Nesir--associated with the eagle-god, Nisroch) portrayed a victorious battle and the bull (Shur) as the slain.

In the constellation Sagittarius, the image of the god Jupiter is found symbolized in the form of a "bull" [Taurus; he who is Jah], the opposite of the "eagle" in Scorpius. Jupiter, as the bull, was worshipped under the constellation of the Ram, over whose head is Deltoton, the triangle, by the ancients considered a sacred, mysterious, and divine emblem. Jupiter (in Greek, Zeus) is another name for Jove, a corruption of Jehovah.

There is a somewhat obscure reference to Revelation 6:1-2, found in II Kings, *"And the king of Assyria brought men from Babylon, and from Cuthah, and from Ava, and from Hamath, and from Sepharvaim and placed them in the the cities of Sammaria instead of the children of Israel. "*

Ephraim and Manasseh were two of the 12 tribes of Israel that initially populated the Northern Kingdom of Israel with Samaria as its capital.   The early Samaritans' and the Sepharvaims' worshipped, among their many deities, a god named Anammelech, meaning "Anu is king" (II Kings 17:30-31). Anammelech and Adrammelech, meaning "Adar-Molech" (see II Kings 19:37) were typically portrayed as "white horse-gods," and still rendered as such in Hermetic and Kabbalistic allegories. More importantly, Anammelech can be traced to Baal or Moloch [Nimrod] worship with symbolic imageries depicting the Northern sector of the heavens in the realm of Sagittarius.

Now refer back to Rev. 5:11, *"And I beheld, and I heard the voice of many angels round about the throne and the beasts and the elders; and the number of them was ten thousand times ten thousand, and thousands of thousands. "*—compare Rev. 5:11 with both Daniel 7:10 and Jude 1:14, which reads, *"And Enoch also, the seventh from Adam, prophesied of these saying, Behold, the Lord cometh with ten thousands of his saints. "* What picture is Jude giving here? It is a picture of the 6,000 years allotted to mankind before judgment of the ungodly (vs 15). This same time-period was depicted in Deuteronomy 33:2 in the 12 tribes of Israel and the *"fiery law."*

When Moses blessed the tribes of Israel, he rendered a joint blessing to the children of Joseph, Ephraim/Manasseh, and in this message was a distant depiction of the last days (Deut. 33:13-17): *"His glory is like the firstling of his bullock"* [Taurus being the 1st of the Vernal Equinox during the time of Abraham]. Remember, the Aleph and the bull, Aleph meaning "the first" and bull meaning the "strong one." *"...and his horns are like the horns of unicorns...."*

Unicorns are mythological creatures with one-horn, but Deuteronomy speaks of "horns" in the plural sense. Some translations such as the old Revised Version of the Bible render unicorns as "wild ox" (see also Psalm 92:10), but again there is no such animal as a one-horned, wild ox. If this passage is read in the symbolic context of Hebrew cosmology, it becomes very clear that "unicorn" represents the Aquarius (Ephraim) and Capricorn (Manasseh) sector of star constellations. The unicorn, standing as "one" or "powerful one," was one of the ancient symbols found on the crests of the Kings of Israel, and today, a similar crest can be found on the coat of arms of Great Britain. Earlier renderings for Capricornus associate it with the "horned sea goat."

HORNED HEAD OF ALEXANDER THE GREAT.

A similar reference can be found in Deut. 33:13-17, *"...with them he shall push the people together to the ends of the earth:"* These are the people of the last days, *"...and they are the ten thousands of Ephraim, and they are the thousands of Manasseh"* (Deut. 33:13-17). Here again is this same reference to "thousands and ten thousands" of people in reference to the last sector of the Hebrew time-clock located in Aquarius/Capricorn. These star constellations are considered as Ephraim/Manasseh and joined together under Joseph symbolizing the 6,000 years of the time-line.

First Ephraim and then Manasseh: This is the same order the 12 tribes of Israel marched in their wilderness journey arrangement, and also found on the banners (or ensigns) of the 12 tribes. "Judah, Issachar, and Zebulun marched together (first; Numbers 10:14) from the East side under Judah's standard (the lion of Leo) (Numbers 2:3; Numbers 26, 1 Chron. 2-8); under Reuben's standard (Taurus the bull) on the South marched Reuben, Simeon, and Gad; under Ephraim's standard (Aquarius, the man) on the West marched Ephraim, Manasseh, and Benjamin. The Midrash, Pesikta Rabbati (3:93), makes reference to the fact that Ephraim was always before Manasseh (see below where Ephraim comes before Manasseh just as the Vernal Equinox moves from right to left). Under Dan's standard (Scorpio, the serpent and/or the eagle) on the North marched Dan, Asher, and Naphtali (Numbers 2). In the midst of the camp, center, were the Levites; *"...as they encamp, so shall they set forward, every man in his place by their standards"* (Numbers 2:17)."

The following list arranges the 12 Tribes according to camp layout in Numbers 2-4, and star constellations according to the calendar of time-periods:

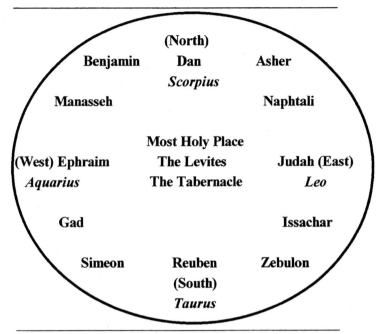

A reference can be found in Hosea 13:15 that addresses the tribe of Ephraim and obviously this inference can be applied to the stars of the constellation of Aquarius:

> *Though he be fruitful among his brethren,*
> *an east wind shall come, the wind of the*
> *Lord shall come up from the wilderness,*
> *and his spring shall become dry, and his*
> *fountain shall be dried up; he shall spoil*
> *the treasure of all pleasant vessels.*

Ephraim was aligned to the West (Hosea 11:10), opposite the Tribe of Judah in the East, but also the "east wind" refers to the Assyrians (Hosea 12:1). Everywhere in ancient symbolism, Aquarius has been associated with water as "a fountain or spring" being poured out from a "vessel." In the Egyptian zodiac and the Latin translation, the word Aquarius represents the "urn" and the act of water rising, sending forth.

This same end-time scenario can be seen in Mark 14:12-16 when Jesus sent forth "two witnesses," *"Go ye into the city, and there shall meet you a man bearing a pitcher of water: follow him."* This picture reveals the time-period of Ephraim/ Aquarius, "the water bearer."

The tribe of Ephraim (the fountain) in the West was located opposite Judah (the lion, Hosea 13:7-8) in the East. In the preceding chapter, Hosea reveals the idolatry of Ephraim, *"...when he offended in Baal, he died"* (13:1-2), and *"Judah also shall fall with them"* (Hosea 5:5). This was the prophecy in II Kings 17 about the children of the house of Joseph, Ephraim and Manasseh, who founded the Northern Tribal section of Israel (and who would later come into captivity from Assyria because of Idolatry), *"Ephraim shall be desolate in the day of rebuke: among the tribes of Israel have I made known that which shall surely be"* (Hosea 5:9); and *"When I would have healed Israel, then the iniquity of Ephraim was discovered, and the wickedness of Samaria"* (Hosea 7:1; see also Hosea 9:17).

ASSYRIAN BATTLE SCENE.

Jeroboam was from the house of Joseph-Ephraim, the largest tribe in the Northern Kingdom, symbolic of the name for the entire Northern Kingdom—and yes, symbolic for all of those redeemed *"out of every kindred, and tongue, and people, and nation* (Rev. 5:9).

Now compare Daniel 7:10 with the above scripture passages: *"A fiery stream issued and came forth from before him: thousand thousands ministered unto him* [the saved remnant], *and ten thousand times ten thousand stood before him* [the unbelievers]: *the judgment was set, and the books were opened."* All of these scriptures pertain to the coming judgment of the ungodly, and the judgment at the End of the Age. Jeremiah confirms this time-period of judgment when he writes, *"Yea, the stork in the heaven knoweth her appointed times; and the turtle and the crane and the swallow observe the time of their coming, but my people know not the judgment of the Lord"* (8:7). In studying Daniel 7:10 closely, it becomes obvious a far greater meaning in the words, *"fiery stream."*

In the Talmud, Chagigah 13b, a "fiery stream" means the Milky Way! Here the Milky Way has been referenced specifically in conjunction with the time of both the judgment and the End of the Age. Remember, Daniel 7:10 reads, *"A fiery stream issued and came forth from before him...."* The center of our galaxy is in the direction of the constellation Sagittarius.

A similar reference can be found again in the book of Job 38:31-33, in reference to the Mazzaroth, *"Canst thou bring forth Mazzaroth in his season?...,"* refers to a "star cluster" within the zodiac and this cluster is the Milky Way. More importantly the Vulgate translation uses the term for the Milky Way in connotation with Lucifer, *"...or canst thou guide Arcturus with his sons?"* If you combine all of this with the scripture reference in Revelation 6:2, *"I saw a white horse, and he that sat on him had a bow...and he went forth conquering and to conquer,"* it paints a symbolic picture of the number

"666" occurring in the time-period of the constellations of Sagittarius and Scorpius (more on "666" later).

This explanation reveals the one who sits on the white horse with crown and bow, known as Centaur (Cheiron) by Aratus and Eratosthenes as the "horseman and beast." The white horse of the 1st Seal reveals the false prophet and anti-christ as the "image of the beast."

The Book of Ezekiel 8:5 reads, *"Then said he unto me, Son of man, lift up thine eyes now the way toward the north. So I lifted up mine eyes the way toward the north, and behold northward at the gate of the altar this image of jealousy in the entry."* Again, the man of Scorpius (aka the likeness of Nimrod, a Babylonian symbol) at the Winter Solstice and the Northern sector of the circle represented in the images of Tammuz and the abominations of the 12 signs of the zodiac.

The man of Scorpius, or 666, is also the great deceiver. He will come to deceive and to verify himself through the prophecies which foretell of the greatness of the true Messiah. A clearer picture of this man comes in a description of the remainder of the Four Horsemen:

The Red Horse

First, the "white horse," then each of the other seals follow consecutively, opening one after the other, through the time-period indicated by Scorpius, known to Aratus as "the great beast" and found in Revelation 6:3, the color of the red horse which equals the symbols of "war" with rivers of blood (Isaiah 63:2; Rev. 12:3).

War, the 2nd Seal, is the result of the 1st Seal (Dan 7:24; 11:40-45; Matthew 24:6-7) when peace is taken from the Earth. The 2nd Seal aligns with Jesus prophecy of "wars and rumors of wars." Wars will erupt all over the world. Israel, and specifically Jerusalem, will be the central focus, because Jerusalem is the center of the world (according to the ancient Rabbins), and it will be Jerusalem where the anti-christ will establish his throne. Jerusalem is God's Holy City of old, prophecied throughout the Old and New Testament.

It will also be Jerusalem where the "abomination of desolation" will be placed. The abomination of desolation being the corruption of the temple and the Holy of Holies.

The Black Horse

The 3rd Seal, the black horse, reveals the result of war and violence: "famine." Famine comes from the scarcity of food, rationing of supplies, provisions, etc., and an imbalance of economical conditions (Lam 5:10; Jer 4:28; Jude 13).

The balance of power is held in the hands of the one who conquers—the anti-christ; and it is the anti-christ who will hold the power over both governmental powers and religion. He will undertake a great plan to send throughout the entire world disciples and armies, *"...partly by persuasion and mighty miracles, partly by threats and open force, he may constrain the whole human race to yield to him, and to receive his yoke."* *(12)*

And how could the anti-christ proceed with his plans unless he has a group of innumerable individuals who are morally united in one, common (anti)spirit against the purposes of God? This purpose and definition can be found in 1 John 4:3: **"And every spirit that confesseth not that Jesus Christ is come in the flesh is not of God; and this is that Spirit of Antichrist, whereof ye have heard that it should come; and even now already is it in the world."**

Interestingly, the Vulgate (through reasoning of Scriptures) mentions this passage as *"Every spirit which dissolveth (the bonds of) Jesus: qui solvit Jesum.*—This being none other than the apostatizing from the faith, and would certainly satisfy the goals and definitions for the anti-christ as a person or even as an opposing system of belief. From the evidence of John's writings, this opposing system of belief had

already begun in the world, and of which Paul also revealed,
"For the mystery of iniquity doth already work."

In great detail, Ibn Ezra concludes with his findings on
the anti-christ gathered from a variety of early scholars: *"Some
add, that Satan shall unite himself in such a way to him, that
Antichrist shall not be purely man, but a man-
devil...[unnaturally conceived]...he shall...have no guardian
angel, but Satan himself; of whom Antichrist shall learn all
kinds of divinations and magic, by which he shall perform
prodigies in the world...The place of his birth, and the
beginning of his greatness, will, they say, be Babylon, in whose
ruins, and in whose neighbourhood, shall be settled, if not all
the tribe, at least some family of Dan...."*

According to Ibn Ezra, it will be in Babylon where the
Antichrist, as a full-grown man, will declare himself "The
Messiah" and begin to perform many miraculous works, and it's
all worth quoting here:

*"His fame thereof being soon spread abroad the Jews
shall fly from all parts of the world, and from all the tribes, to
join themselves to him, and offer him their services. Seeing
himself acknowledged as Messiah, and adored by all the tribes
of Israel...he will set out with that formidable army to the
conquest of Palestine; which shall instantly surrender, with
little or no resistance.   The twelve tribes shall return, and
establish themselves in the land of their fathers, and in a short
time shall build for their Messiah the city of Jerusalem; which
shall be the capital, or court of his universal empire.   After
Antichrist shall have conquered Jerusalem, he shall, with great
ease, conquer the rest of the earth, if, indeed, he have not
conquered it before going to Jerusalem...With this view, he
shall prohibit, by the severest penalties, not only the worship
of false deities, but chiefly the worship of the true God of his
fathers, and above all, the exercise of the Christian religion.
Whereupon shall arise, the most terrible, the most cruel, and
the most perilous persecution against the church of Jesus
Christ; and it shall last for three years and a half...Several*

things remain which are not so interesting, as his name, his character, his physignomy, his particular miracles, and the precise time in which he is to appear in the world, which many have dared to define. Time has already falsified the most of those prognostics, amongst which one still remains to be falsified, to wit, that of Juan Pico Mirandulano, who promises Antichrist against the year 1994."

NOTE: End-time Babylon has been the subject of much controversy as to whether or not the Bible describes the "real" city of Babylon or a "symbolic" system of the original Babylon. Much would depend on whether or not the Bible is taken literally as to the term "Babylon" in describing the actual city located in the country of Iraq;   figuratively, in describing a system of government; or the symbolism of the Anti-Christ's ultimate evil influence over the entire end-time world.   The latter being representative of "mystery" Babylon (Rev 17:5), and associated symbolically with an evil, spiritual empire first established by the precepts of the actual city of Babylon.

This could be a matter of confusion for many because Revelation 17 and 18 describe a literal place where the anti-christ reigns, a worldly kingdom known as Babylon.   In contrast, the Bible indicates that Babylon would be completely destroyed, never to be reinhabited or rebuilt as the same magnificent city that once stood as a mighty, powerful empire amidst the civilizations of the ancient world (Isaiah 13:7-22; 47; Jeremiah 50, and Revelation 17, 18).

The original city of Babylon has been thoroughly destroyed from its original majestic state, but the Bible clearly states that the "seeds" of Babylon's deception would not be destroyed until the day of the Lord. God pronounced judgment against Babylon, because Babylon became the seat of idolatry, **"...for by thy sorceries were all nations deceived"** (Rev. 18:23).

The black horse can be found in the pair of balances associated with the star constellation Libra which in early cosmology was found connected to the "claws" of Scorpius.

Greed will fuel the desires of people on earth, *"...a measure of wheat for a penny..."* and it will be most of the wealthy of the earth who align with the anti-christ in efforts to preserve and further their materialistic empires. The precious remnant, the few existing among the corrupt majority, can be seen in the symbolic expression, *"...and see thou hurt not the oil and wine,"* and similarly found in Ezekiel 13:19: *"And will ye pollute me among my people for handfuls of barley and for pieces of bread, to slay the souls that should not die, and to save the souls alive that should not live, by your lying to my people that hear your lies?"*

The Pale Horse

Famine brings death and pestilence which are found in the 4th seal, the pale horse, also connected to the stars marked by the time-period of Scorpius (Libra including Virgo). The stars of Libra and Virgo are included here because at one time they were connected to the stars of Scorpius. A circle consists of 4 quarters. If you remove 1 quarter (1/4) there still remains 3/4; but more descriptively, if you carve out a section of the circle beginning with the stars of Aquarius to Scorpius, you have removed 1/4 part of the circle.

"...And power was given unto them [Death and Hell] *over the FOURTH part of the earth, to kill with sword, and with hunger, and with death, and with the beasts of the earth"* (Rev. 6:8:). Power was given to Death and Hell in the personification of the destruction wrought by the hands of the anti-christ and his followers. Also, notice that "power" was given to "them." In other words, given by permission. Here, Death and Hell are representative of Satan; later, Judgment is representative of God.

The 5th Seal "Ara," the altar, is clearly in heaven identified within the constellation of Sagittarius. *"...I saw under the altar the souls of them that were slain* [martyred] *for the word of God"* (Rev. 6:9) during the period of the anti-christ. The ancient symbols associated with Ara, the altar, under Sagittarius, are depicted with shooting flames as it receives the marytred. Here again, the martyrs for the Word of God (as a result of the first four seals) are symbolically associated with the Lamb who was slain (Rev. 5), and pictured differently than those returning with the Conquering King in Revelation 19:11 (see also Psalms 74:5, 9, 10; 89:46; 94:3,4).

The martyred cry out from the "altar" of sacrifice for vengeance *"...on them that dwell on the earth?"*—Vengeance here because the final judgement of the wicked has not yet come. To these souls were given *"...white robes..."* and *"...it was said unto them, that they should rest yet for a little season, until their fellow servants also and their brethren, that should be killed* [martyred] *as they were, should be fulfilled"* (vs. 11).

The ominous 6th Seal begins the vengeance of God in Judgment upon the wicked just before the opening of the 7th Seal and introduction of the last 7 Trumpets. In the first 5 Seals, the Lamb granted permission to the anti-christ to finish his destruction before the 6th Seal began the time of Judgment.

The wrath of God is first felt upon the earth, then poured out upon the heavens, *"And the heaven departed as a scroll when it is rolled together..."* (vs. 14). The heavens depict "time," and when the heavens are rolled together, "time" is no longer.

Lastly, at the end of the 6th Seal, Judgment is seen against those who rejected the truth of the Righteousness of God in Christ Jesus, *"the kings of the earth, and the great men, and the rich men, and the chief captains, and the mighty men hid themselves in the dens and in the rocks of the mountains..."* (vs. 15).

The 6th Seal marks the beginning of the end of the Ages depicted in God's wrath. *"...and, lo, there was a great earthquake; and the sun became black as sackcloth of hair, and the moon became as blood...For the great day of his wrath is come; and who shall be able to stand"* (Rev. 6:12-17; see also Joel 2:30,31; Isaiah 13:9,10; 34:4).

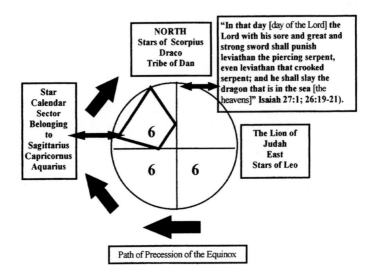

NORTH
Stars of Scorpius
Draco
Tribe of Dan

"In that day [day of the Lord] the Lord with his sore and great and strong sword shall punish leviathan the piercing serpent, even leviathan that crooked serpent; and he shall slay the dragon that is in the sea [the heavens]" Isaiah 27:1; 26:19-21).

Star Calendar Sector Belonging to Sagittarius Capricornus Aquarius

The Lion of Judah
East
Stars of Leo

6

6   6

Path of Precession of the Equinox

Why would the people of the earth, both great and small, hide in rocks and dens? Because it isn't the anti-christ who they hide from, but the wrath and judgment of the Lamb of God. They rejected salvation through Jesus Christ, as the slain Lamb who is about to return as Victorious, Conquering King (see Deut. 32:39-43; Matt. 24:29; Heb. 10:28-31).

The 7th Seal marks the beginning of the 7 Trumpets, and the 7th Trumpet includes the 7 Vials which bring the final judgment and culmination of Time.

What can be evidenced in the Seven Seals is the period of time marked between the stars of the constellation of Aquarius through Scorpius. The Seven-year Tribulation period spoken of in the Bible (Matthew 24:36-37), indicates a specific period of "time," and it is likened to a period of "seven" Jewish years or 2,520 days [7 years x 360 days = 2,520 in approx. Jewish years].

The beginning point of this 2,520 year time-span calculated by many Christians begins when the anti-christ *"confirms the covenant"* with the people of Israel (Daniel 9:27; 12:11-12; Rev. 11:2-3; 13:5). This time-period will be known as the "time" of Jacob's trouble or the Tribulation. Here again you find the PE and the Six Great Ages of Mankind. The PE takes 2,154 years (averaged at 2,000 years, or one "age") to move through each one of the 12 divisions before returning to its original point of calculation.   Isn't it interesting how close the numbers "2,154" and "2,520?" The closeness of these numbers are no mere coincidence.

Now look at another example: 360 days x 70 years = 25,200 days [the time it takes the PE to move one full circle through the 12 constellations] or 25,200 days divided by 12 months of the year = 2100 [one Age]. (Or 360 days x 7 years = 2,520). The figure 25,200 closely   approximates the total circumference of the land for the priests and Levites in Ezekiel 48:8, *"and the sanctuary shall be in the midst of it"* (Ezek. 48:20; Jer 25:11). The circumference of the land in Ezekiel aligns almost exactly to the circumference of the earth. Again, are these numbers merely a coincidence?

The Bible tells of a man who slowly attains great leadership, emerging on the scene of a world in chaos, and will convince many that he is the promised messiah the world has been awaiting. The leopard has always been a symbol for a bold, aggressive, conquering power and typifies the likeness of Nimrod (nimar, nimr) (Daniel 7:6; Rev. 13:2, 11). Nimrod is a symbol of the false Messiah.

If Leo symbolizes the First of the Lion of the Tribe of Judah on the East, or the Messiah, then there must be the opposing force, and this opposing force is represented as the "dragon" (Draco containing the ancient Pole Star location of Thuban) on the North west - as in the sign or season of Sagittarius/Scorpius (Rev. 12:3). Why? Because there is a geographical, mathematical map of the true, and the false is represented by the 12 Signs of the Zodiac established by Nimrod (read Ezekiel). One as like Nimrod, the dragon, the beast (along with his many other names), is typified as the anti-christ (Rev. 13:1, 2, 12:9, 11-16). He can be found in the number of a man, one like Nimrod, and in his number, 666 (Rev. 13:18).

In regard to the number 666, Irenaeus wrote, *"the greatest diligence has been applied to the deciphering of this enigma."* Numerous names have been given to describe the man represented by the number "666" from Domitian, Nero, Napoleon, Stalin, Hitler, the Pope, various kings and even Presidents. Revelation 14:18 indicates, *"...Let him that hath understanding c-o-u-n-t the number of the beast...."* Clearly, the number 666 is mathematical, and some people have attempted to explain this as simply a number "9" viewed as an upside down "6." When combined it would reveal the triplicity of the number 666, but there is little else to substantiate this viewpoint.

Another method is to interpret the Greek numerals to form a word or name for 666; but the problem here is the letters, when combined, form an innumerable variety of proper names from both ancient history up to modern times—not to mention the fact that the beast is numbered, not named. Out of all the various methods for calculating the beast's name, which one is the true name? The learned scholar Calmet responded to the futility of the latter way of calculating the number when he wrote, *"Verily a vain study, and profitless marks, to which perhaps we should repent of having given so much of our attention."*

So how will anyone know the beast, or the anti-christ, or his mark? A much clearer explanation can be found by understanding the time-line of both history and the Book of Revelation. If the beast is not specifically named, then both he and his followers fall into a different category that can only be determined by numbers and periods of time:

In an earlier chapter, the Six Great Periods of Time were shown to align with the Solstice/Equinox points. It takes "6" months from the Summer Solstice of the stars of Leo, as the likeness of the Sun (or Son), arrived at the point of the Vernal Equinox of the bull, stars of Taurus, and "6" months from the bull of Taurus to the Autumn Equinox of Aquarius, the man, and "6" months from Aquarius, the man, to the stars of

Scorpius, the corrupted eagle now "the dragon" in the 12 constellations - when added together equals the number "666."—still not convinced?

The six periods of Time equal 1/4 of the constellations or three constellations of 2,000 years each.   The Six Great Periods of Time give us an indication of the End of the Age, but also the identification of the number 666.   Who is the beast or dragon of the 12 constellations? It is the number of the man of Sagittarius/Scorpius! Look for one who imitates Christ, but represents the Babylonian Nimrod!   Again, this can be compared to the true map of the constellations being countered by the worship of Nimrod's 12 signs of the zodiac in astrology. When is the End of the Age? If we follow the outlined map of the Ages, then it would occur sometime at the point when the Vernal Equinox appears in Aquarius and the Winter Solstice occurs in Scorpius! This time-period is pictured in the graph on Page 118.

Now return to the Book of Ezekiel 8:5, *"Then said he unto me, Son of man, lift up thine eyes now the way toward the north. So I lifted up mine eyes the way toward the north, and behold northward at the gate of the altar this image of jealousy in the entry."* Again, the man of Scorpius (aka the likeness of Nimrod, a Babylonian symbol) at the Winter Solstice and the Northern sector of the circle represented in the images of Tammuz and the abominations of the 12 signs of the zodiac. *"And he brought me to the door of the court...So I went in and saw; and behold every form of creeping things, and abominable beasts, and all the idols of the house of Israel; portrayed upon the wall round about...Then he brought me to the door of the gate of the Lord's house which was toward the north; and, behold, there sat women weeping for Tammuz"* (Ez. 8:7-16).

Tammuz is a "type" of Nimrod, and Nimrod is a "type" of the anti-christ. And what better way to describe the anti-type of the beast than in Isaiah 14?

---

*How art thou fallen from heaven, O Lucifer, son of the
morning! how art thou cut down to the ground* [Rev. 12:7-
9], *which didst weaken the nations* [through idolatry and
worship of the heavens]*! For thou hast said in thine heart*
[pride], *I will ascend into heaven* [the throne room of God], *I
will exalt my throne* [the zodiac-astrology] *above the stars of
God* [the true use and meaning for the star constellations]*: I
will sit also upon the mount of the congregation* [equality
with God], *in the sides of the north* [Scorpius, the Tribe of
Dan]; *I will ascend above the heights of the clouds* [to
conquer God's throne]*; I will be like the most High* [the anti-
christ covets the place of God].

The prophecy of Revelation reveals that the seals will
be broken and begin their fulfillment when the Vernal Equinox
arrives at the beginning sector of the star-based calendar at zero
degrees of Aquarius.

The reason for this, again, would be the result of the
P.E. It takes approximately 2,000 years for the P.E. to move
through one star constellation. The P.E. has moved 2,000 years
through the star constellation of Pisces, and is about to enter
Aquarius.

From the zero point of the star calendar in Aquarius to
midpoint would equal 1,000 years. This would be equivalent to
the 1,000 years of the Millennium. Remember, Rosh
HaShanah is also known as the "opening of the gates of
heaven," and correlates with the 7,000th year, the Millennial or
Sabbath rest at the end of the time-line for the Ages. This is a
depiction of the resurrection.

And so, the culmination of the wedding banquet is found
in Luke 12:35-37 , when it reads, *"Be dressed ready for
service and keep your lamps burning, Like men waiting for
their master to return from a wedding banquet, so that when
he comes and knocks they can immediately OPEN THE*

DOOR for him. It will be good for those servants whose master finds them watching when he comes."

The Seven Seals are revealed by the time-period marked in heaven from the P.E. in Aquarius through Scorpius (1/4 sector of the circular calendar of prophecy as seen on pg. 118).

The First Seal - White Horse - Pegasus in Aquarius
> the rider & the bow - Sagittarius
> the crown - Kronos - Nimrod (type)

The Second Seal - Red Horse
> a great sword - Sagittarius/Scorpius

The Third Seal -Black Horse
> The stars of Libra connected to Scorpius

The Fourth Seal - Pale Horse
> 1/4 part of the Earth represents 1/4 part of the circle of time from Aquarius - Scorpius
> Death and Hell

The Fifth Seal - Ara - Sagittarius
> The Martyrs

The Sixth Seal - Scorpius
> The wrath of God
> Judgment

The Seventh Seal - The culmination of Time marked by the Stars of Aquarius through Scorpius

An Ancient Secret; A Corruption of Truth

In the ancient names depicting the 12 chief deities of Graeco-Roman mythology, the Roman name of DIANA is the feminine for the the Tribe of Dan, meaning "ruler," and ARTEMIS is the Greek, meaning "who cometh." The Roman name, Diana, and the Greek name, Artemis, are found depicted in "the circle of 12 gods" representing (the feminine side of) Sagittarius. In ancient prophecy, this sector of the heavens between the constellations of Aquarius and Scorpius was known as "the window."

The window has a very, very important two-fold meaning: to the early Messianic Christians this was the "the window" or "doorway" to heaven associated with the "resurrection, catching away, or rapture." The Romans borrowed the idea which came to be associated with the "Roman god of beginnings." Now, the Roman god of beginnings was Janus, the door god, whose counterpart was the feminine, Jana. Jana was another name for DIANA (remember in the above paragraph Diana was the feminine side of Sagittarius). The Roman temple of Janus was shut in universal peace, because Janus means peace or rest.

The reason the "doorway" is so very important is because it marks the passageway through to the outer heavens, and was blocked by Satan until the time of the Messiah. Jesus Christ "opened" the "doorway" to heaven through his life, death, and resurrection, but this sector of the heavens is still part of Satan's domain until the final judgment. AND this is where the "false christ" will be described in prophecy.

Herodotus explains that even the Egyptians borrowed this ancient prophecy because the *"...Egyptian priests told that after 3000 years, the dead would rise again."* An end-date for the world, more in alignment with the Bible, was calculated from the Egyptian zodiac of Denderah, and hinted at in the configurations of the Egyptian pyramids. It is in the constellation of Sagittarius where a doorway would open to the outer heavens. Also, according to ancient Mayan legend, the end of the world will occur at the Winter Solstice in the darkest sector of the constellation of Sagittarius in A.D. 2012, when the Solstice point conjuncts the Milky Way and Sagittarius.

The ancient Rabbins gave the Hebrew root   for   the constellation of Sagittarius as "Heth" (or "Cheth")   П
and means "Terrorem" or "Terror." A later Hebrew noun for the constellation Sagittarius interpreted "Cheth" as "a living animal (beast)" (see Genesis 1:30).

The planets, Jupiter and Saturn, have anciently been assigned to the anti-christ's "reign of terror." "Satur," "Satr," or "star" are the ominous names associated with Saturn (Latin meaning hiding), and Saturn is another name for Satan. Saturn was known in Arabic as Zohal or Refan meaning hiding, sheltering, or resting. In the Egyptian, Jupiter and Saturn were interchangeable and called Seb or Sabbatei (also known among other names as Phaethon, Phainon or Nemesis).

Interestingly, in the ancient Hebrew, Saturn also represented "rest," (Hebrew, Sabbatei) but it was a time of rest for the righteous associated with the Sabbath, the 7th Day Rest, and the Millennial "rest" of the 7,000th year. As detailed earlier, Nisroch, the eagle-headed human, is an emblem for the heavenly sector of Sagittarius/Scorpius, sometimes depicted as the winged-sun disk. The name, Nimrod, also belongs to this sector of constellations, and Nimrod comes from the Semitic root "marad," meaning "to rebel."

The Sagittarius/Scorpius constellations have been assigned by the ancients to the Seat of Satan, as god of this present age and lord of the northern black void. He was known as the ancient serpent in the Garden of Eden; lord of idols, prince of false gods; a 7-headed sea monster known as Leviathan; Nimrod, the king of Babylon; the Phoenician King of Tyre, and prince of the power of the air (Eph. 2:2) where he ascends to the "north" in Isaiah 14, to overthrow God, establish his throne, and thereby rule over the entire universe.

The oldest of legends tell of the end of the Age at the "end" of the 6000th Millennium, but even though we are close, no one really knows precisely when that will occur. Remember the problems with the calendar? As it stands today, prior to A.D. 500, it becomes very difficult to match precise dates, unless someone has developed a computer program containing a Nautical Almanac, star catalogue, and proceeds to calculate dates counting backwards from Solar eclipses and other celestial events that were recorded in early history.

As an example, the following include just a few of the interpretations of those who undertook the process of calculating a time-period counting the years from Adam to Christ. They are based on the 6,000 year time-line as referenced in the book, "The Magi: In Search of Messiah," Shirley Ann Miller, 1999, pg. 93):

From Adam to Christ:

Alphonsus	6,984 years
The 70 translators	5,199
Albumazar	5,328
Hales	5,411
Jackson	5,426
Ussher	4,004
Petavius	3,983
King James Bible (161 1	4,004
Christian calendar	4,000

From Adam to Present:

Hebrew, Rosh HaShanah of 1999   5,760
Aleph b'Tishrei
(Mishnah, San Hedrin 38b) based on the
Book of Genesis (Bereishit) or "in the beginning"

A 15th Century Rabbi foretold the Second Coming of Meshiach benDavid would occur during a spectacular celestial showcase that occurs at the end of this Century. This would be obvious in the form of several different celestial phenomenon. One being the Cherubic formation found in the four-square shape of the constellations of Taurus, Aquarius, Scorpius, and Leo of both Ezekiel and Revelation marking the introduction into the next Millennium (see Page 52). A similar conjunction of this type occurred in August of 1999 and will be repeated in May of 2000. Sometime after this event, the heavens would birth a giant comet/meteor (coming from the Sagittarius/ Scorpius constellations) which would purposely plot a destructive course toward Earth (see Revelation 13,

"Wormwood"--Wormwood is an herb associated with paralysis and death).

The great, Roman historian/philosopher, Pliny the Elder, described this event as "a terrible comet" having a "fiery appearance." -- Interestingly, in July of 1995, the gaseous comet "Hale-Bopp" was observed traveling through the constellation Sagittarius (now Capricornus due to the P.E.). Many thought this to be the infamous "Wormwood" comet of prophecy.

What makes this time-period so significant is the fact that the ancient patriarchs of the Bible "prophecied" of this four-square alignment thousands of years ago. Every prophetic time-period written in the Bible aligns with this same configuration in history, and as the Bible has truly revealed history in times past, so it also reveals the future in prophetic time-periods.

Planetary alignments and most celestial phenomenon are not rare, and neither are eclipses such as the one that occurred on August 11, 1999 (Av 29, 5759), just East of Jerusalem; but the same configuration of stars, planets, weather patterns, comets, eclipses, etc., (and Y2K) at the end of a Century should be considered as quite profound. Could these wondrous displays from the heavens reveal a sign from God? Is it possible that the time-patterns of heaven cry out with the impending prophecy of Revelation revealing the end of a "season" and the transition into a new time-period of the 7,000th year?

In a moment, in the twinkling of an eye, at the last trump; for the trumpet shall sound, and the dead shall be raised incorruptible, and we shall be changed." ! Cor. 15:52

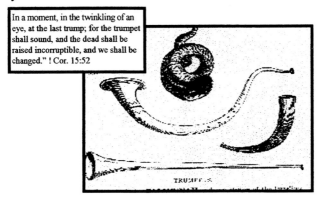

TRUMPETS

CHAPTER VIII

THE 144,000, TWO WITNESSES, AND SUN-CLAD WOMAN

"And after these things I saw four angels standing on the four corners of the earth, holding the four winds of the earth, that the wind should not blow on the earth, nor on the sea, nor on any tree" (Rev. 7:1).

The 6th Chapter of Revelation ends with the events occurring in the 6th Seal, but the 7th Seal doesn't begin until Revelation 8.   Revelation 7-18 pertain to past, present, and future time-periods. These time-periods are presented with major headings, and introducing the first of these is the representation of the 144,000 in Revelation 7.

The 144,000

Revelation 7 presents a parenthetical pause.   This parenthetical pause reflects upon the 144,000, a great multitude of people standing before the Throne of God, and the angels, elders, and four beasts about the Throne.

There is a slight difference between the martyrs of the 5th Seal and the multitude referenced in Revelation 7. The 5th Seal martyrs are among those redeemed from the earth prior to the Great Tribulation— "the souls under the altar who wear white robes and wait for their brethren to be killed."

The 144,000 in Revelation 7 are the ones who "came out of great tribulation" and are a symbol of the remnant from the 12 Tribes of Israel established at the time of the promised Covenant with Abraham/Jacob's descendants.   Abraham's Covenant was a witness to the entire world the evidence of a One, True God.   This time-period encompasses the Covenant promise from beginning, captivity, disbursement, to reunification (past, present, and future) and includes the remnant (symbolic 144,000) out of the 12 Tribes all the way to the end of the Great Tribulation.—This number represents all of the 12 Tribes redeemed from the Earth, and by the blood of the Lamb symbolized by the number 144,000.

The symbolic remnant of 144,000 is parenthetical and derived by multiplying the 12 Tribes of Israel by the representative 12,000 from the entire time-span of the Earth (the latter being the entire circle of time.) This symbolism represents an undeterminable number, just as Abraham/Jacob's seed would be as the sands of the sea - infinite in number.   The time-periods revealed in Revelation 7 consist of:

♦   24 hrs [elders] = 1 day (or) 2,000 years x 12 time periods represented by the 12 tribes - 24,000 years (or)

360 days per year x 2,000 years per age = 72,000

72 hrs = 3 days (or) 72,000 years x 3 days = 24,000 (or)

72,000 hrs x 2 (72 hrs of 3 days) = 144,000 Sealed

144,000 (of 12 Tribes) divided by 24 (elders) = 6,000 years

God told his children they would not be appointed to wrath (wrath being judgment, not martyrdom), and the angels were instructed not to hurt the earth until the entire remnant, all of God's people, are sealed with His promise.   There are a number of ways to demonstrate this example:

(1)   God protects the 144,000 (all those redeemed) against His wrath and judgment (Rev. 9:4);

(2)   The Great Tribulation saints were a "great multitude, which no man could number, of *"ALL nations, and kindreds, and people, and tongues..."* (vs. 9). The 144,000 is symbolic of all of the 12 Tribes of Israel who migrated and settled into all nations of the world. This number curiously excludes Dan from among the 12 Tribes.

(3)   The elders (of time), those gone before, asked who all of these people were and where *"whence came they?"* (vs. 13);

(4)   The angel said, *"These are they which came out of great tribulation..."* (vs. 14);

(5)   These great tribulation saints (the symbolic 144,000), serve God in his temple and God "shall" dwell (Tabernacles) with them. God only "dwells" (vs. 15) with His bride after the Marriage Supper (Rev. 21:1-11).— Compare Rev. 7:15-17 with Rev. 21: 3-6. They can also be seen in Revelation 21:17, in the measurements of the New Jerusalem as a symbol for the totality of the redeemed.

Here again in Revelation 7:1, *"the four corners of the earth"* are represented in heaven by the four star constellations of Leo, Taurus, Aquarius, and Scorpius (the four beasts; see Page 52). It is the shape of a cross. In Verse 5, the number of 144,000 from the 12 tribes were sealed, and note: This list differs from the Genesis 35 and 46 accounts.   Dan was not included in the list of tribes because his share was given to Ephraim and Manasseh named under the tribe of Joseph. Ephraim and Manasseh are included in the 12,000 of the Tribe of Joseph, just as Aquarius and Capricornus are considered joined in time.

The 144,000 in Revelation 5-8, represent the final "Ages" of mankind, but include all of the martyred during the Great Tribulation (7:14). This number can be found in I Kings 19:18, during the days of Elijah when God reserved the 7,000 prophets (depicting the 7,000 years of time) who remained faithful witnesses, marked by God, who did not bow their knee to Baal.

The "parenthetical" sealing of the 12 Tribes obviously represents the symbolic time-period encompassing the entire span of history assigned to the children of the promise? For example: 144,000 divided by 24 hrs = 6,000 years. NOTE Daniel's 70 weeks: 360 years (= times) x 2 = 720 (= time) divided by 1/2 time of 360 years = 180 (= 1/2 of time) added together (360+720+180) equals a total of 1260. Or, 360 x 7 = 2,520 (1,260 x 2 = 2,520; 2520 divided by 7 = 360).

Another way to look at this would be 1260 x 2 = 2520 equals approximately "one age" (1260 divided by 30 months = 42 months; 42 months = 3 1/2 years). The number 1260 represents one-half of an age. Rounded, these numbers equate to 1,000 (one half age) and 2,000 (an age) (70 x 7 = 490 years = 500th year is the Year of Jubilee). You will see the number 1260 referenced in Revelation 11:3 and 12:6 (also see also Daniel 7:25; 12:7).

The 144,000 can be seen in the Feasts, meaning "set times," telling us the time of things to come (Col. 2:17). God establishes His "time periods" depicted over and over again throughout scripture as evidence of prophecy fulfilled. When God established the Old Testament Feast of Pentecost he established a "set time" which occurred 50 days after the Festival of Firstfruits. This prophetic time-period was fulfilled again in the New Testament in Acts 2 at the Feast of Pentecost in the "sealing" of the Apostles 50 days after the Festival of Firstfruits. Likewise, God sealed the 144,000 from each of the 12 tribes in Revelation 7:3-8.

This coming together of all the 12 Tribes is also symbolically evident in Ezekiel's vision of the dry bones.— compare Ezekiel 37 (specifically vs. 9-10 here) with Revelation 7.

From Revelation 7 to Revelation 14 reveals this time-period in history. In Revelation 7, the symbolic 144,000 are seen from the standpoint of the Great Tribulation *"standing before the throne"* (vs 7:9), while the 144,000 in Revelation 14 have been redeemed from the earth, sealed with *"...the Father's name written in their foreheads"* and appear with the Lamb as a mighty army stands awaiting battle (14:1). They will be the 144,000 *"redeemed from the earth"* who were among *"the firstfruits unto God and to the Lamb"* and symbolically portrayed as the army accompanying the Conquering King, Jesus Christ at the Second Coming (no longer symbolically represented as a Lamb) in Revelation 19:14 (see Ezekiel 38-39 in comparison).

The symbolic 144,000 here are the victorious remnant throughout history who have not been defiled with women [spiritual virgins] awaiting the hour of judgment upon the world (vs. 6 and vs. 13).

The Tribe of Dan

Iben Ezra associated the tribe of Dan as the one blotted out (Deut. 29:18-21) because of idolatry. Perhaps, because of idolatry and the golden calf (symbolic of star worship) worshipped by the tribe of Dan at Bethel (I Kings 12:25-30). The golden calf is symbolic of Egypt (a type of sin) and the corruption of God's time-line in the constellations into the worship of the stars/planets through astrology.

This comparison can be found in Jeremiah 8 when God judged Judah for her sins of idolatry in worshipping the heavens (Jer. 8:2), and in the subsequent Babylonian invasion of Judah, *"The snorting of horses was heard from Dan"* (Jer. 8:16). The city of Dan was the farthest towards the NORTH and originally named Laish. It was conquered by the Tribe of Dan (the Danites) who changed the name to that of their father (Judges 18:27-31). But it is a little known fact the Tribe of Dan, the Northern Kingdom of Israel (the Southern Kingdom was Judah), also migrated along the southern shores of the Caspian Sea gradually moving still farther NORTH. They eventually became emersed among the northern Europeans (the Northlanders; Anglo-Saxons), Russia, and Poland. From this migration evolved the name for one of the most important rivers in all of the European community, "the Danube River." The name of the Danube comes from the name Dan, and the Tribe of Dan were amongst the noblest of ship builders and sailors (Judges 5:17).

Early scholars, such as Ibn Ezra, believed that the exclusion of one of the Tribes among the 12 in Revelation only adds proof that the anti-christ will emerge from the Tribe of Dan. Interestingly, the Tribe of Dan corresponds to the exact position of the stars of Sagittarius/Scorpius in the great time-clock of man as the *"serpent by the way"* (see Jacob's blessings for his children in Genesis 49).

Further proof of Ibn Ezra's claim can be found in a reference made by Ezekiel (21:25-27) in regard to the end times (vs.25) when he writes, *"...and thou, profane wicked prince of Israel, whose day is come, when iniquity shall have an end, Thus saith the Lord God; Remove the diadem, and take off the crown."* This passage of scripture gives further proof of the princely identity of the number 666 and the anti-christ.

First, God uses Babylon as a sword of judgment against Judah, and then judgment is used against Babylon. This is how it will be for the great prince who is likened to Nimrod, the founder of Babylon (the Son of Perdition), but who will be accepted by the Jews as the Meshiach benDavid. This false "crowned" prince, who will *"die the deaths of the uncircumcised"* (Ezek. 28:10) can be identified through his description found in the constellation of SAGITTARIUS near the edge of the Milky Way in the stars known as Corona Australis or THE SOUTHERN CROWN (aka the Centaur's Crown), and further referenced in Ezekiel 28:2-10 with the *"Prince of Tyrus."* *"Because thine heart is lifted up, and thou hast said, I am a God, I sit in the seat of God* [in the North], *in the midst of the seas* [the heavens].... *"*

According to Ezekiel (8:13-14), this wicked Prince is covered in precious stones (the false temple) and exalts himself above God (Dan. 11:36-37).

The 4 beasts and the period of time from Abraham to Messiah can also be found in a comparison between Revelation 7:17, Ezekiel 47, and the New Jerusalem. *"For the Lamb which is in the midst of the throne shall feed them, and shall lead them unto living fountains of waters: and God shall wipe away all tears from their eyes"* (Rev. 7:17).

Ezekiel writes of the 4 corners of the earth with a circle as the circumference of the sanctuary: *"Afterward he brought me again unto the door of the house; and, behold, waters issued out from under the threshold of the house eastward: for the forefront of the house stood toward the east"* (Ezek. 47:1).

The river flowed from the right (stars of Leo), the east to the south (stars of Taurus) side of the altar (from right to left; east to west). The man measured a literal 1,000 cubits 4-square [the 4 beasts of Revelation] and back to *"the brink of the river."* The man with the measuring rod measured the equivalent time-span of 4,000 years (see Page 52).

Following the "parenthetical" sealing of the 144,000 comes the Great Tribulation saints worshipping around the Throne of God in heaven (Rev. 7:9-17), and then begins the 7th Seal with the Seven Trumpets (Rev. 8:1-13; 9:1-21). The 7th Seal brings forth the vengeance prayed by the martyrs of the 5th Seal and the judgment of God upon the wicked. This prophecy can be followed in Revelation 8-9:

- 1st Trumpet: hail, fire, and blood cast upon the earth 1/3 of the trees were burnt up and all of the grass upon the earth;
- 2nd Trumpet: the sea became blood; 1/3 of the sea died;
- 3rd Trumpet: a falling star burned up 1/3 of the rivers;
- 4th Trumpet: sun, moon, and stars darkened; only 1/3 part of the light continued to shine;
- 5th Trumpet: a star falls from heaven with the key to the bottomless pit; tormenting of those without God's Seal upon their foreheads

♦ 6th Trumpet: the time-period that was prepared for this hour, day, month, and year to kill 1/3 part of mankind.

During the sounding of the Trumpets, 1/3 of the waters of the earth, 1/3 of the heavens, and 1/3 of mankind will be destroyed.

The Mighty Angel and The Two Witnesses
Time-Period and Subject: Second Coming and The End of Time

A parenthetical pause occurs between the 6th Trumpet and the 7th Trumpet between Revelation 10 and before Revelation 12. The mighty angel of Revelation 10 has a very important mission. He declares in a loud voice, *"that there should be TIME no longer..."* (vs 6-7). Why is this passage so very important?

In Verse 2 and 5, the angel with a little, opened book stood with his right foot on the sea and left foot on the earth. Confusing?—not if you understand the verses in conjunction with verses 6 and 7 (above) and the 7,000 year time-line. In Revelation 10, the angel was announcing the end of the 6,000 years of time just prior to the beginning of the 7,000 year, *"and when he had cried, seven thunders* [7,000th year] *uttered their voices"* (vs. 3). In this passage, the Book of Revelation gives us a specific period of time, *"...in the days of the voice of the seventh angel, when he shall begin to sound, the mystery of God should be finished, as he hath declared to his servants the prophets"* (vs. 7).

What direction will Jesus Christ split the sky in the Second Coming? In the East, as the rising of the sun (vs. 1). When the angel faced west standing with his back to the east, he placed his right foot on the sea (Scorpius) and his left foot on the earth (Taurus)—in a star-based calendar Scorpius and Taurus reveal the Equinox and Solstice points towards the end of time. They are the keepers of Time and Seasons of the earth, as we know it.— The angel announces "that there should be time no longer. The movements of the heavens stop.—As a result, Time ceases (Rev. 21:23; 22:5).

John was then told to eat the little book because the beginning of the 7,000th year would be delayed. There was still work to be done on earth, *"Thou must prophesy again before many peoples, and nations, and tongues, and kings"* (vs. 11). These are the martyrs of the Great Tribulation.

Chapter 11: The Two Witnesses
Time-Period and Subject: The Great Tribulation For Unbelievers, A Season of Rest for Believers

All Scripture should blend and interact with other Scripture throughout the Bible, and this would include the Book of Revelation. Thus far, it should be obvious that the Moses' Wilderness Sanctuary, the Jewish Feast days, the Ages of the Church, and the New Testament references harmonize together. Therefore, Chapter 11 should flow in this same manner with the entirety of Scripture.

John was told by the angel to measure the temple of God, *"And there was given me a reed"* (see Eze 40:3), but John was on the Isle of Patmos so how could he literally measure the temple of God? The measuring of the temple was not the earthly temple, because the Temple in Jerusalem was destroyed in A.D. 70, approximately 25 years prior to the writing of Revelation. The temple John was to measure was the New Jerusalem and the "spiritual" temple of the Lord (see Eph 2:19-22; Rev. 21:1,9, 21:15). The temple referenced here was the one in heaven which will be comprised of the saints.   These are the saints of Revelation 6:11, who *"rest yet for a little season..."*

The measuring reed is also a tool of judgment (Isaiah 11:4; Micah 6:9) distinguishing between good/evil and between only those who were permitted to enter into the inner court. This example compares to the days of Temple worship when only the priests and Levites were permitted entrance "versus" in the New Jerusalem when only the redeemed and chosen may enter the Kingdom of God.   It is also seen in Psalm 52:8 where it is obvious the difference between good and evil, between the judgment of the ungodly and the blessings experienced by the just, *"But I am like a green olive tree in the house of God"* (see also Zech. 3:1-10; Haggai 2:19). The inner and outer court represent the saved versus the unsaved.

The temple, the altar, and the worshippers are symbolic of Moses' Tabernacle in the Wilderness (Ex. 29:44, 45). The outer court in Revelation 11 was for the Gentiles [in comparison to the unsaved] who shall *"...tread under foot forty and two months"* (42 months) (vs 2) (see II Chronicles 23:4-6, Luke 21:24, Romans 11:25). *"Jerusalem shall be trodden down of the Gentiles, until the times of the Gentiles be fulfilled"* (Ezek. 21:27). The two witnesses will *"prophesy a thousand two hundred and threescore days, clothed in sackcloth"* (1260 days) (vs.3).

42 months = 3 1/2 years

1,260 days (vs. 3) divided by 30 months = 42 mos.

1,260 x 2 = 2,520 (Rev. 11:3 and Rev. 12:6)

2,520 divided by 7 = 360 or 360 x 7 = 2,520

Although 42 months is the same as 1,260 days, these two numbers have two different meanings referring to two different time-periods. The 1,260 days in Revelation 11:3 begin in B.C.E. 520 with the prophet Zechariah's call to "repentance" for the remnant (perhaps numbered in the thousands) who would prepare spiritually to build the temple. In Revelation 11:3, the witnesses are wearing sackcloth as a sign of repentance. Zechariah had God-given visions which pertained to the present post-exile remnant through the ultimate fulfillment of prophecy that would be evidenced in the Coming of the Messiah. This period of repentance was symbolized in Revelation 11:3 as 1,260 days (years). This was a message to the chosen remnant of the 12 Tribes of Israel. The 42 months of Revelation 11:2 refer to the Great Tribulation (Zech 12:3-10).

——The prophets, Zechariah and Haggai, preached the call for repentance and the laying of the Second Temple foundation beginning in B.C.E. 520 (approx.) (Haggai 1:8).

Jerusalem is depicted in Scriptures as not only a city but a group of people who reside within the New Jerusalem. The two periods of time (the olive trees) represent the Old Testament Jews (1,260 years; a symbolic remnant of the 144,000) and the New Testament Saints (Rev. 12; 1,260 years) as they become united into one to become the Bride of Revelation. When combined, the two olive trees symbolize not only a time-period but the "Whole House of Israel" (Romans 3:24; 9:25-26; 11:17; Zech 2:11, 10:6). According to Ephesians 3, all of this will be accomplished in the "dispensation of the **fullness of times**" when God will gather in **one** *all* things in Christ" and this will happen when **time is no longer**.

John provides a deep spiritual inference when he reveals that the two witnesses represent both the fulfillment of prophecy and the reign of the Messiah over all of the earth (the lampstands). This prophetic time-period is calculated beginning in B.C.E. 520 with the call to repentance until the coming of the Messiah which was to occur at the end of 2,520 years (1,260 - Rev. 11:3 + 1,260 Rev. 12:6 = 2,520) (see Haggai 2:15-16). It is a matter of simple mathematical calculation to subtract B.C.E. 520 from 2,520 years which equals **A.D. 2,000** (approx) or **A.D. 2,001,** if including the year "zero" between B.C.E. and A.D. as counting for one year.

Another way to look at this would be from an earlier reference to the 144,000 (all of the remnant) using the following equations: If you measure 360 days x 7 weeks, the equivalent is 2,520 days (years). The number "7" means "completeness." Another example is: 360 days x 70 years = 25,200 days. The 25,200 days (years) represents the time it takes for the Precession of the Equinox to move one full circle through the star calendar of constellations. The number 25,200 closely approximates the total circumference of the land for the priests and Levites in Ezekiel 48:8, *"and the sanctuary shall be in the midst of it"* (see also Ezek. 48:20), as well as the circumference of the earth.

Of course, it is understood that this calculation of B.C.E. 520 is based upon the times given according to the translation of the King James Bible (1611). If the times were translated incorrectly, then the calculation would be inaccurate. This only proves that "no man [specifically] knows the day or the hour." God in His Wisdom has granted us the knowledge of the SEASON for the Second Coming, and it will most likely occur during Rosh HaShanah (the Feast of Trumpets) in the year A.D. 2,000, 2001, or + "?." And Zechariah confirms this when he wrote, *"And the Lord shall be seen over them, and his arrow shall go forth as the lightning: and the Lord God shall blow the TRUMPET, and shall go with whirlwinds of the south" (Zech. 9:14, 14:5).* Whatever the Time, be mindful, the Season is very near!

A PERSONAL NOTE: On a personal note, I believe it will come at a time when the evils of the world will grow unbearable. Many new souls will come into the Kingdom and many souls will depart from the Faith. God has always chosen a "remnant," and the 144,000 is an example of this.

The witnesses of Revelation 11 are true prophets who testify of the coming judgment of God wearing sackcloth, the symbol for repentance. The Greek word "euaggelion" means "declared" or "testify" and where the word evangelism is derived. Revelation 11 is a time-period just before the 7,000th year, or Millennial rest. The time-period occurs during the 42 months (or 3 1/2 years) of Revelation 11:2, a time of rest for the saints and the Great Tribulation for the nonbelievers (represented by the time-period mentioned in Rev 10:11; see also Dan 12:7). John reveals this in verses 1 and 2. The saints are sheltered (Zech 2:5) and worship in the temple, but it is the outer court and the holy city that will be *"tread under foot...."*

In John 3:14-22, the angel of the Church of the Laodiceans writes, *"These things saith the Amen, the faithful and true WITNESS, the beginning of the creation of God..."*

Who is the Amen?   Amen is the Word of God, *"In the beginning was the Word, and the Word was with God, and the Word was God"* (John 1:1).

The Bible tells us that (1) the Word of God is a witness, and (2) that John the Baptist was *"...a man sent from God, whose name was John. The same came for a WITNESS, to bear WITNESS of the Light, that all men through him might believe. He was not that Light, but was sent to bear WITNESS of that Light"* (John 1:6-8).

The two witnesses of Revelation will be two witnesses of the Word of God, and just as John the Baptist came to bear witness of the Light, the First Coming of Christ, the final two witnesses of Revelation will come to bear witness of the Second Coming.—And just as Zechariah and Haggai represented the two witnesses concerned with the rebuilding of the Temple in Jerusalem after the captivity, the two witnesses of Revelation testify to the Throne and Temple of God in the New Jerusalem (see Ezra 5:1-2).

This association can be further understood by studying a few of the parallels between the Book of Zechariah (revealing the Millennial temple) and Revelation 10-12 (revealing the Throne of God). The almost identical comparisons prove that Revelation 11 and 12 were borrowed and repeated, in part, from the prophet Zechariah:

♦ Zechariah: proclaimed the kingdom of God is at hand; the golden candlestick and 2 olive trees (4:11); the measuring line (2:1-2); the flying scroll contains the judgments(5:1-2); and the Messiah will return "east"of Jerusalem with His feet on the mount of Olives facing "west" (14:4); here Zechariah depicts Jerusalem's future glory under the Messiah.

♦ Revelation: 2 witnesses proclaiming the judgment of God; the 2 candlesticks and 2 olive trees (11:4); the measuring reed (11:1); the little book contained the final judgments of God (10:2, 8-11); and Jesus Christ, the Messiah, will return "east" of Jerusalem facing "west" (10:2) (see also Matthew

24:27); here Revelation 10-12 reveals the Millennial reign of the Messiah to establish His Kingdom.

The candlesticks of Zechariah are similar to the lampstand in the Mosaic tabernacle. One candlestick represents Jesus Christ (the Light of the world), and the other candlestick represents the Holy Spirit. The two olive trees are the 2 witnesses to the Light.

Remember in the Jewish wedding, the two witnesses had to actually "see" the groom coming before they made the announcement to the bride (and the groom usually came at night; 1 Thess 5:1-2; Matthew 25:6). This also compares to the sighting of the new moon on the first day of the month [Rosh Hodesh] which must be verified by "two witnesses" before the announcement of THE BEGINNING of the Feast of Trumpets (or Rosh HaShanah) could begin.

The presence of the two witnesses of Revelation 11:3 have verified the timing of the Second Coming. They are given power to speak prophecy [a declaration of the coming judgment], to work miracles, to miraculously defend themselves, to release plagues, and to finish their testimony. On the Feast of Trumpets, the 7th Day Trumpet of God will sound the Jubilee, and Jesus Christ [the groom] will descend *"...with a shout, with the voice of the archangel, and with the Trumpet of God; and the dead in Christ shall rise first. Then we who are alive and remain shall be caught up together with them in the clouds to meet the Lord in the air"* [the bride] (1 Thess 4:16-17; Lev 25:8-10; Zech 4:1-11; 9:13-17; Rev. 11:15).

The 7th Trumpet (vs.14-19) announces the 7,000th year, *"The kingdoms of this world are become the kingdoms of our Lord and of his Christ; and he shall reign forever and ever."* This passage of scripture follows the fulfillment of Revelation 10:7. Rosh HaShanah is also known as the "opening of the gates of heaven," and correlates with the 7,000th year, the Millennial or Sabbath rest at the end of the time-line for the Ages (Rev. 11:18-19).

And so, Luke 12:35-37 reads, *"Be dressed ready for service and keep your lamps burning, Like men waiting for their master to return from a wedding banquet, so that when he comes and knocks they can immediately open the door for him. It will be good for those servants whose master finds them watching when he comes."*

The time-period revealed in Revelation 11 with the two witnesses is 1260 (1/2 of an Age or near approximate to 1,000 years) is as follows:

(1)   The time-line for Revelation 10-12 is revealed in Zechariah beginning with the Second Temple in B.C.E. 520. The time-line passes from the Old Testament to the New, and the time-period was divided into two segments of 1,260 years (Rev. 11:2-3; Rev. 12:6, 14) ending 2,520 years later which will be after approximately A.D. 2,000 (or 2,001+).

(2)   The court that John measures is the Millennial court in Jerusalem, and those redeemed from the earth are already worshipping in the Temple. The people in the outer court are left out. They must endure the Great Tribulation. They are among the Gentiles who were deceived (Rev. 20:8) and who come with the beast after he is released from the bottomless pit to encompass "the camp of the saints." This is portrayed in Zechariah, *"And many nations shall be joined to the Lord in that day...and I will dwell in the midst of thee"* (vs. 2:11);

(3)   This can be viewed another way: The two witnesses testify of the Second Coming of the Lord to those unbelievers who dwell on the earth for 42 months just prior to the Millennium; the two witnesses are the believers among those in the "first resurrection." The rest of the dead *"lived not again until the thousand years were finished"* (Rev. 20:5).

Revelation 11 is a capsulated version of Revelation 20 where the saints received their rewards and the nations left on earth (outside the inner court) were angered against God (Rev. 11:18). At this time (after the Millennium), Satan will be released to deceive the nations and they will come against the

Holy City (Rev. 20:9) and the people of God to fight (Gog and Magog).

(4)   *"For God hath not appointed us to wrath, but to obtain salvation by our Lord Jesus Christ"* (I Thess 5:9). The Day of Atonement (or Judgment) follows the Feast of Trumpets and fulfills the Promise that believers in the Messiah, the Church, were not appointed to wrath (or judgment), and thereby completes the Age of the Church. The Day of Atonement is also known as the "closing of the gates of heaven." Then follows the Feast of Tabernacles which is likened to the Marriage Supper of the Lamb.

(5)   Only the two witnesses are mentioned as belonging to God, where are the rest of the believers? The only other people left on the earth are the unbelievers, and they are the ones who hate the two witnesses for pronouncing judgment upon *"them that dwelt on the earth"* and *"their enemies beheld them"* as they ascended up to heaven Rev. 11:2-12). It was only after a great earthquake when a "remnant" *"gave glory to the God of heaven"* (vs. 13).

(6)   The beast "ascends" out of the *"bottomless pit."* This is also found in Revelation 11:7, when John writes "after" the two witnesses have finished their testimony, the beast ascends and makes war with them (see Rev. 9). An example of this can be found in Revelation 12:7-9, where the beast is first pictured in heaven before he is cast to earth, and in Revelation 13:5-6, where the beast blasphemes God for 42 months. The same as in Revelation 11:2, and not only does the beast blaspheme God but also His **"tabernacle, *AND THEM THAT DWELL IN HEAVEN"*** (13:5-6).

   The ones dwelling in heaven are among the inner court of Revelation 11:1-2.   Revelation 13 occurs during the time-period of Revelation 11, *"And all that DWELL UPON THE EARTH shall worship him* [the beast] *whose names are not written in the book of life of the Lamb slain from the foundation of the world"* (Rev. 13:8).

(7)   The two witnesses are a part of the numbered in the *"first resurrection"* and *"on such the second death hath no power"* (Rev. 11:8-12; 20:6).

(8)   The time-period of the two witnesses compares with the time-period the woman flees into the wilderness.

Rev. 11: 1260/42 months/3 1/2 years

Rev. 12: 1260/42 months/3 1/2 years

The woman is protected in the wilderness for 1,260 days (3 1/2 years, Rev. 12:14) during the Great Tribulation of Revelation 11. The "remnant" the serpent persecutes during the 42 months will be those who became a part of the "chosen few" who came to Christ during the Great Tribulation.

In Revelation 10:7 the "seventh angel BEGINS to sound," but in Revelation 11:15, the "seventh angel SOUNDS. This passage of Scripture is a picture of the Second Coming of Jesus Christ with His judgments and His rewards.

Chapter 12 - The Sun-Clad Woman

Time-Period and Subject: Jerusalem, The Church, The Covenant

The beast of Revelation 11:7 appears in Revelation 12, but parts of Revelation 12 actually should appear before Revelation 10 in sequence. Confused? The beast of Revelation 12 appears in heaven and is cast to earth (see Dan. 8:10). This is a picture of the first 3 1/2 years which actually depicts the birth of our Savior, Jesus Christ, while Revelation 11 is a picture of the last half of the 3 1/2 years (3 1/2 x 2 = 7), and Revelation 10 reveals the end of Time. The beast is in heaven before he is assigned to the bottomless pit.

"And there appeared a great wonder in heaven; a woman clothed with the sun, and the moon under her feet, and upon her head a crown of twelve stars" (vs. 1).

Clearly, this passage of Revelation is presented in astronomical symbolism, but first and foremost, should be the determination as to the identity of the "sun-clad woman with the crown of 12 stars." Many scholars throughout the years have represented "the woman" mentioned in verse one, as Israel, but it should become more obvious when reading further that the "woman" more specifically represents "Jerusalem," and the compilation of the crown of 12 stars symbolizes all of Israel's 12 tribes.

To the Jewish people, and throughout the Bible, Jerusalem has always been considered to be the "center of the Earth." *"The land of Israel is at the center of the world; Jerusalem is the center of the land of Israel; the Temple is the center of Jerusalem." (14)* And as Jerusalem is portrayed as the center of the Earth so it is considered to be typified in the heavens as the center of God's kingdom mentioned in the New Testament references as the *"New Jerusalem"* coming down from heaven (Rev. 3:12; 7:1; 10; 21:1-2; 22:14-15). Jerusalem shall be called the throne of God, *"...and all the nations shall be gathered unto it, to the name of the Lord, to Jerusalem..."* (Jer. 3:17).

Jerusalem has been called "the holy city" (Rev. 21), and the tabernacle or throne of God, descending out of heaven. The 12 gates of the city corresponded to the 12 tribes and 12 apostles. The 4 walls are constructed on 12 foundations and have 12 gates (12 x 12 = 144). Notice the woman of Revelation 12:1 is centralized while being clothed around her by the sun, and as is well-known, the sun is the center of our solar system.

In Revelation 12:1, the word *"stephanos"* (translated crown) is a garland (or wreath) indicating victory. It is not the word for *"diadema,"* or "diadem," which symbolizes the crown of royalty. The woman in Revelation 12 indicates one who has arrived victorious from battle. The crown of 12 stars represents the 12 tribes of Israel just as the New Jerusalem is surrounded by the 12 gates with the names of the 12 tribes of Israel, and the wall has 12 foundations with the names of the 12 apostles, so the crown of 12 tribes (stars) surrounds the woman's head (New Jerusalem) as a victorious crown.

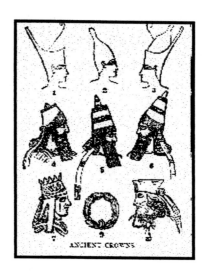

ANCIENT CROWNS

The New Jerusalem can also be found evidenced in the last chapter of Ezekiel, where a different division of the holy land is depicted than what was presented in the time of Joshua. The earlier holy land division located the tribes of Judah, Benjamin [Jerusalem and the Temple] farther South (Ezekiel 40:2). Ezekiel reveals the division of the Promised Land, among the remnants of the 12 tribes of Israel, as a future event, and the tribe of Judah (Jerusalem) is now placed in the middle of all the tribes [just as the New Jerusalem of Revelation is depicted as in the center] with the holy land extending much more to the South.— Rather than unequal portions in reference to size and location, Ezekiel's depiction is perfectly equal over all the tribes, all lying four-sided from East to West with its height far to the East of the sea until it terminates in the sea itself.

Jeremiah 3:6, refers to Israel as a "backsliding nation" and the bride (here Israel) was given a "bill of divorce and put away" (Isa. 50:1). God's presented His mercy to Israel (as a people) to turn from their sins of idolatry and repent (vs. 12-14).

If they turned then God would bring them to "Zion," and both Israel and Judah would be as one. If you look at vs 17, *"At that time they shall call Jerusalem the throne of the Lord, and all the nations shall be gathered unto it...."* Clearly, Israel and Judah are presented as nations, but Jerusalem is still separated as a distinct place, a city. Now compare Jer 3:17 with Rev 21:3, a tabernacle and throne are synonymous, and a tabernacle and throne are always in the "center." Jeremiah distinctly refers to both Israel and Judah as nations of people, and Jerusalem as a city (see Jeremiah 14-20).

In Isaiah 60, Israel, Judah, and the Gentile nations, are all brought together *"...And the sons of strangers shall build up thy walls..."* (vs 10). Now what is Isaiah referring to in vs. 14, *"...The city of the Lord, The Zion of the Holy One of Israel?"* Here again, Zion and Jerusalem are interconnected as a distinct place (Jerusalem), but also as a name for the people who inhabit it, *"...and they shall call thee..."* (see Rev. 14:1). If you compare Isaiah 60:11 and 19 with Revelation 21:23-25, *"Therefore thy gates shall be open continually....and....The sun shall be no more thy light by day...."* - this is Jerusalem, The Holy City of God.

In following this same thought, compare the above passage with Isaiah 61:10, *"I will greatly rejoice in the Lord, my soul shall be joyful in my God; for he hath clothed me with the garments of salvation, he hath covered me with the robe of righteousness, as a bridegroom decketh himself with ornaments, and as a bride adorneth herself with her jewels."* Also, look at Isaiah 62:3, *"Thou shalt also be a crown of glory in the hand of the Lord, and a royal diadem in the hand of thy God."*

Here we find a diadem, or crown, universally known as the symbolism for royalty or authority as is the woman crowned in Revelation 12. The difference is in the Isaiah reference, the woman is royalty, but in the Revelation 12:1, the woman is both royalty and victoriously crowned. Clearly, this reference speaks to the bridegroom adorned ready to receive his bride, and clearly, Jerusalem is depicted as the crowned woman of Revelation 12 (see also Isaiah 62:1-7; 2 Kings 11:12; Est.2:17).

Also, one might question: "How can Jerusalem be represented as a chaste virgin and when only the Church is represented as a virgin?" Then read Isaiah 62:5 in speaking of Jerusalem: *"For as a young man marrieth a virgin, so shall thy sons marry thee: and as the bridegroom rejoiceth over the bride, so shall thy God rejoice over thee"* (see also vs. 6, 7, 10)....and in verse 12, *"And they shall call them, The holy people, The redeemed of the Lord: and thou shall be called, Sought out, A city not foresaken."*

Isaiah 66 should make this even clearer: *"A voice of noise from the city, a voice from the temple, a voice of the Lord"* - a voice from Jerusalem, from the Throne of God, from the voice of the Lord! Again Rev 12:1 can be seen in Isaiah 66:7: *"Before she* (who? Jerusalem) *travailed, she brought forth; before her pain came, she was delivered of a man child."* Compare this to Revelation 12:2: *"And she being with child cried, travailing in birth, and pained to be delivered."*

If one states, "Israel [not specifically Jerusalem] brought forth a man-child," it conflicts with Scripture. Because Israel did not bring forth a man child, JUDAH DID: Isaiah 65:9: *"And I will bring forth a seed out of Jacob, and out of Judah...."* Guess where the capital of Judah was in the Old Testament?— And guess where the Church was born on the day of Pentecost (Acts 2)?— And where will *"all the people of the Lord"* of the Earth go to worship? To the tabernacle, the throne, *"...to my Holy Mountain Jerusalem..."* (Isaiah 66:20). (see again Isaiah 66:22 and compare to Revelation 21:1)

Again, Chapter 21:2 describes the bride, the new Jerusalem. The bride is the holy city of Jerusalem *"coming down from God out of heaven, prepared as a bride."* (see Rev 21:9-27). Here again, Jerusalem is compared to a tabernacle (see 21:3) (as in the center). When compared the rest of scripture it gives a clearer understanding of Revelation 12 and the identity of the Sun-Clad Woman.

Clearly, the woman of Revelation 12 and the city of Revelation 21 speaks of "Jerusalem," and those who reside there are the chosen, victorious "remnant" (i.e., the symbolic figure of 144,000) of all tribes, nations, peoples, and includes the New Testament Saints.

The victory has come in several ways, but one of the most easily referenced and most important comes from Genesis 3:15, *"And I will put enmity between thee and the woman, and between thy seed and her seed; it shall bruise thy head, and thou shalt bruise his heel."* Genesis reveals the chasm of sin created by the curse of disobedience unto God, but Revelation 12:17 depicts a war-torn remnant of the woman's seed, *"which keep the commandments of God, and have the testimony of Jesus Christ."* In the beginning, the serpent appeared to have won the battle over the seed of the woman in Genesis, but the remnant seed of the woman in Revelation, prevails to conquer the serpent and win the war in the end.

Jesus Christ has won the victory, and his story from birth, death, and resurrection is briefly told in Revelation 12:1-5. Here He awaits, poised and ready for the Second Coming (Rev. 14:1).

In Revelation 12:6, the woman flees into the wilderness for 1,260 days (years), and this picture aligns with same time-period of 1,260 days (years) in Revelation 11. This again, is a picture of the entire time-span from B.C.E. 520 until A.D. 2000- "?" —It is a picture of the Millennium Rest for those in Christ and likewise, a picture of the Great Tribulation for the unbelievers.

Revelation 12:7-9 reveals a great battle where Satan is cast to earth to deceive the entire world and this can best be depicted from Isaiah 14:9-20, specifically vs. 12-14, *"How are thou fallen from heaven, O Lucifer, son of the morning!"* *["and the dragon fought and his angels, And prevailed not; neither was their place found any more in heaven. And the great dragon was cast out, that old serpent...which deceiveth the whole world," Rev. 12:7-9]* And what did Satan say in his heart, *"I will ascend into heaven, I will exalt my throne above the stars of God* ["...And his tail drew the third part of the stars of heaven..." Rev. 12:4]: *I will sit also upon the mount of the congregation* [Jerusalem; *"And he opened his mouth in blasphemy against God, to blaspheme his name, and his tabernacle, and them that DWELL IN HEAVEN"*], *in the sides of the north* [the stars of Scorpius; the 7,000 year; the 7th Angel, Rev. 11:15]; *I will ascend above the heights of the clouds; I will be like the most high...."* [Now is come salvation, and strength, and the kingdom of our God, and the power of his Christ: for the accuser of our brethren is cast down..." (Rev. 12:10)]

   And who were the overcomers? These were the remnant "seed of the woman" who were persecuted for their belief in Jesus Christ (Rev. 12:13-16), and who *"...overcame him by the blood of the Lamb..."* (Rev. 12:11). These are the ones in the Millennium who *"...rejoice, ye heavens, and ye that DWELL IN THEM..."* (Rev. 12:12) because Satan is cast down to the earth to deceive the nations, *"Woe to the inhabitants of the earth and of the sea"* (Rev. 12:12). This is another picture of the difference between the redeemed (preserved) and the unbeliever (judged) who must endure the Great Tribulation (also compare Rev. 12:13-16 with Isaiah 17:12-13, 59:19-21; and Dan 7:18, 22, 27).

Did you know ... that Jerusalem has been leveled to the ground five times and changed hands twenty-six times? Throughout history, various nations have desecrated the beloved city and turned it into a city of destruction...but,

Did you know ... that Jerusalem is Promised and proclaimed by God Almighty as the Eternal City of King David and Capital of the Nation of Israel?

Did you know ... that Jerusalem is mentioned **657** times in the Tenach (Bible), and **154** times in the New Testament.

HINDOO REPRESENTATIONS OF THE UNIVERSE

CHAPTER IX

WHO IS THE GREAT RED DRAGON, THE FIRST AND SECOND BEAST?

Rev. 12:3: *"And there appeared another wonder in heaven; and behold a great red dragon, having seven heads and ten horns, and seven crowns upon his heads."*

    If the first wonder (vs 1-2) was astronomical, then why wouldn't the second wonder be depicted in astronomical symbolism?   Revelation 12 reveals a battle between the forces of God and the forces of Satan, good versus evil. There are two women mentioned symbolically in Revelation, one associated with Jerusalem and the Bride of Christ, and the other, "the mother of harlots" of the city of Babylon (Ch 17).   There are also two other opposing forces: one of the Messiah, Jesus Christ, and the other that of Nimrod, symbolized in a Nimrod-type as Satan or the beast.

    Remember, Leo symbolizes the First of the Lion of the Tribe of Judah on the East, then their must be the opposing force, and this opposing force is represented as the "dragon" or the "old serpent" (Draco containing the ancient Pole Star location of Thuban) on the North West - as in the sign or season of Sagittarius/Scorpius.   NOTE: Draco was also known in ancient history as the "Dragon's Tail." The Dragon's Tail is a meteor shower appearing around May 29, and called the Draconids (see Rev. 4; Job 26:13). *"And his tail drew the third part of the stars of heaven, and did cast them to the earth...* " (Rev. 12:4).

Historically, comets foretold disaster, and in references to a king, foretold death.   Ancient observers noticed when comets approach near the Sun, their tails follow behind them, but as they retreat, their tails appear to go before them.   They viewed the comet's tail as if it pointed down to rest upon the Earth, *"...and the dragon stood before the woman which was ready to be delivered, for to devour her child as soon as it was born"* (Rev. 12:4).

As mentioned before, the Messiah, Jesus Christ, is likened to the Lion of Judah and Jerusalem, Nimrod is likened to the anti-christ, serpent, beast, and Babylon.   Nimrod was known to the Arabs as Orion-al-jabbar, "the giant," a warrior-king who toppled empires and conquered cities, and to the Assyrians he was known as "Cisleu" (the giant).   Actually, according to Augustine, in describing Nimrod, "a mighty hunter before the Lord" is a mistransliteration.   It should read, "a mighty hunter 'against' the Lord."   The Hebrews named Orion, Gibbor "mighty one or the giant" after Nimrod, who they named "kesil" meaning "the fool" because he was strapped to the heavens for rebelling against God.   Nimrod was pictured in the star constellation of Sagittarius/Scorpius.

Nimrod founded his great kingdom of Babel (known as "Bab-ilu," or "Gate of God") which in the Hebrew root was "bll" meaning "to confound," or "balal" "to confuse."

In Mesopotamia, Assyria, and Chaldea monuments have been discovered with carved images of Nimrod with Hoa, the god of water (Pisces, Aquarius, and Capricornus), with a symbolized sacrificial "fish" laid on the altar, and star of Ishtar (Venus), the goddess of love (one of these resides in the British Museum).   Nimrod corrupted the use of the heavens and constellations creating them as a source of worship of him = idolatry.

*Thus in process of time an ungodly custom
grown strong was kept as a law, and
graven images were worshipped by the
commandments of kings...And so the
multitude, allured by the grace of the work,
took him now for a god, which a little before
we but honoured as a man. And this was an
occasion to deceive the world: for men,
serving either calamity or tyranny, did ascribe
unto stones and stocks the incommunicable
name (Wisdom of Solomon, XIII:16-21).*

Instead of Aquarius/Capricornus and other star
constellations depicting the "time" of the Ages, they became
objects of worship, and from the worship of the heavens evolved
astrology.

The eagle, serpent, or dragon were synonymously
associated with the zodiac sign of Scorpius, and sometimes the
symbol of an eagle, serpent, or dragon would be placed on the
Babylonian or Assyrian military standards.

The Red Dragon With Seven Heads, Ten Horns, and Seven Crowns

Revelation speaks of the old serpent as the "devil" and
"satan," but keep in mind, the references to both Jesus Christ/
Jerusalem and Nimrod/Babylon are symbolized through
astronomical associations. Early civilizations ascribed the most
importance to three groups of stars, Arcturus, Orion, and the
Pleiades. Job refers to them as being formed by the Creator,
*"...Which maketh Arcturus, Orion, and Pleiades, and the
chambers of the south* (Job 9:7-9).

The ancient Egyptian god of light was known as
"Shu," but also known as the son of Ra and connected to Osiris
(Apis Bull) and Taurus. The Egyptian Book of the Dead
connects Osiris to the constellation of Orion. To the
Babylonians the constellation of Taurus also represented the
"bull of Anu" and Orion as "Anu's shepherd." —Remember, the
Hebrews associated Orion with Nimrod, "the fool," who was

strapped to the heavens for rebelling against God, and Hesiod also speaks of Nimrod as the strong or mighty Orion in reference to the "mighty one" (gibbor).

Within the northern sector of the star constellation calendar and within the time-clock for the end of the Age, is found the stars of Sagittarius and Scorpius. This is referenced in Isaiah 14:13-14, where the "Northern" sector is depicted as being the location of Sagittarius/Scorpius (see Page 52). But Isaiah describes this area as that belonging to Satan (a personificatiion of Nimrod), and this again is depicted in Job 26, *"He* [God] *stretcheth out the north over the empty place, and hangeth the earth upon nothing...By his spirit he hath garnished the heavens; his hand hath formed the crooked serpent"* (Job 26:7-13).

If the "chambers of the south" (Job 9:9) refer to the stars of the Pleiades, then the opposite stars in the "northern" sector would be those of Scorpius/Sagittarius. The constellation of Sagittarius resides in a rather "empty place" in the heavens. In comparison to other constellations, the stars of Sagittarius appear to be few. Job 26 most likely identifies this relatively empty sector of the heavens before it was known to be Sagittarius. The identification of the "crooked serpent" would be obviously rendered as the star, Draco.

In the New Testament, the Pharisees accused Jesus of casting out devils by Beelzebub and one of the numerous names for Nimrod was Bel (and/or Marduk). The strong man in this instance is "gibbor" and gibbor is referenced to Beelzebub. Here Jesus refers to Himself as the "one" who binds the strong man. Therefore, through a process of deduction one can obviously determine that Beelzebub is also referring to Bel, Marduk, aka Nimrod. This is why the early Hebrews referred to Nimrod as "gibbor."

In other depictions of Nimrod as Hercules (and as Orion), he is represented carrying the world supported on his shoulders. In all accounts, Orion symbolizes pushing, shoving, and force. The rushing, forceful star grouping depicted as a "bull" conveys the coming of the anti-christ as the likeness of Nimrod. The reason, as stated earlier, is because the time-clock of the heavens was corrupted into idolatry. Who is bound in heaven within the depiction of the constellation of Orion? Of course, Satan, Marduk and/or Nimrod, the "bull" of heaven! Who is Arcturus with his [or her] sons? It is the consort deity of Bel Marduk (Nimrod) named in II Kings 17:30, "Ashima," (derivative of "Ash").

One other note worth mentioning is the reference in Job 38:32, *"...or canst thou guide Arcturus with his sons?"* The fourth brightest star in the heavens is Arcturus, and this star appears in the constellation of Bootes. A reference to Bootes and Arcturus, both meaning "to come," can be found in the reference in Revelation 6 with the first four seals. The word Bootes comes from the Egyptian "bau" and the Hebrew "bo."

The star Arcturus in Bootes has long been associated as "the guardian of The Great Bear" (The Great Bear-Ursa Major; Hebrew "Ash" or "Ayish," the congregation of "seven" stars). Some scholars interpret this passage in the feminine rather than masculine gender, *"...or canst thou guide Arcturus with her sons?"* (see also Rev. 13:2), but the "sons" represented in Job are pictured in the heavens as the Great Bear's "tail" [the three trailing stars] or the young following as a tail behind the bear.

The Pleiades resides within the *"chambers of the south"* (Job 9:7-9) in Taurus ("Kesil"-Orion; Spring Equinox during Abraham's lifetime). The Pleiades have been compared to the "seven" stars of Arcturus. Within this constellation, and barely visible to the naked eye, is a group, or cluster, of seven stars located at the shoulder of Taurus called the Pleiades (Hebrew form, kimah or chima, actually a Babylonian name meaning "cluster," and in the Greek known as "seven sailors or seven sisters").

In ancient Babylonian Astrology, the Pleiades, Orion and the dragon, were the gods of the night. Ursa Major and the bison were the Big Dipper (or Great Bear), and the bull (or Taurus) which resides within the constellation of Orion.

This is the star cluster Job referred to when he wrote, *"Canst thou bind the sweet influences* [maedanoth] *of Pleiades* [Chima]*..."* and *"...loose the bands of Orion?"* (Job 38:31). This same group of stars was referenced by Amos 5:8, when he refers to the "maker" of the seven star cluster, *"Seek him that maketh the seven stars and Orion, and turneth the shadow of death into the morning, and maketh the day dark with night...."* "Death" and "morning" refer to the seasonal changes with the rising of the Pleaides in the Spring and the morning setting of the Pleaides in relationship to the Autumn's end (Winter solstice), signifying the end of the crop season. In ancient Babylon, the seven stars in the Pleiades were known as "Sebitti." The warrior gods controlled and dispatched by Marduk to protect Babylon.

The Pleiades came to be associated with the future, death, endings, new birth and beginnings (see Amos 5:8, 21, 26). Human sacrifices were offered to appease the gods. These festivals occurred in November/December in celebration of "endings" with the Autumnal Equinox and Winter Solstice; and again in March/June, during the Vernal Equinox and Summer Solstice ushering in the "beginnings" of the "sweet influences of Spring." Later in history people associated the November Autumnal Equinox with Halloween.

If you combine this story of the heavens, it would become obvious the sign of Taurus actually resides within the heavenly sphere the Babylonians dedicated to their god Nimrod (Taurus) and just so happens to coincide with Abraham's time-line of the Ages. Orion represents the mighty hunter Nimrod and Nimrod, now in rebellion as a deity, finds himself chained in the heavens, bound within the constellation of Orion until he is released to make war upon the world. Nimrod, to the Babylonians, parallels the coming savior of the world. Thus, one might conclude that each of the 12 signs of the zodiac tell a story of Nimrod, and Nimrod is a symbol of the false messiah.

In God's timetable, Nimrod's representation as the anti-christ occurs with the counting of the number 666. The leopard has always been a symbol for a bold, aggressive, conquering power and typifies the likeness of Nimrod (nimar, nimr) (Daniel 7:6; Rev. 13:2, 11).

Revelation 13:1 describes many people as the sands of the sea, and just as Abraham's descendants would be the sand of the sea, these are representative of those who must endure the Great Tribulation, *"...And all that dwell upon the earth shall worship him..."* (Rev. 13:8).   Out of the many nations and people will rise a beast: horn = power and crown = kingship or royalty.   But this powerful ruler is blasphemous and described with the appearance of a leopard whose *"feet were as the feet of a bear, and his mouth as the mouth of a lion; and the dragon gave him his power, and his seat, and great authority"* (Rev. 13:2).   He will rise among the nations as a king seeking to conquer and control the entire world (see Daniel 7-11).

Interesting, that God's throne-room could be described with similar animals as the dragon? Even more interesting is the fact that both are described in astronomical terms! *"And I saw one of his heads as it were wounded to death; and his deadly would was healed; and all the world wondered after the beast"* (vs.3). What is known from Scripture about the dragon, anti-christ and the 1st and 2nd beasts (Rev. 12-13)?

(1)   red dragon was a wonder in heaven;

(2)   the red dragon is described in astronomical terms: 7 heads, 7 horns, 7 crowns (stars of Sagittarius, Scorpius, Draco, the Pleiades, the Lesser Bear in Cancer-Ursa Minor and the Great Bear, Ursa Major); and he has a tail (comet or the tail of the Great Bear), attempts to destroy the child (Jesus Christ) of the woman (Jerusalem/the Church); the dragon was cast out of heaven onto the earth;

(3)   the beast rises up out of the sea (many peoples, nations; but clearly descriptive of the sea or oceans of the firmament; i.e., heaven) with 7 heads, 10 horns, 10 crowns (again the stars); the name of blasphemy (astrology/idolatry);

(4)   the beast was like a leopard (Nimrod/Sagittarius), his feet were like a bear (7 stars of the Lesser Bear in the constellation of Cancer), his mouth as a lion (a counterfeit of the Lion of Judah), the dragon gave him power, seat, and great authority; wounded but healed; and all the world "wondered" after the beast;

(5) he was given great power and worshipped for 42 months (42 months x 30 days = 1260); he has power over ALL that DWELL upon the earth;

(6) the second beast (false prophet) comes from the earth; 2 horns like a "lamb" (again a counterfeit of the true) and spoke like a dragon; he has all of the power of the first beast and causes all to worship the first beast; he performs miracles and wonders in the sight of men to deceive them and the people of earth will be persuaded to make an "image" to the first beast; an image is a "likeness" and the likeness will be both astronomical and astrological; all people must worship the image of the first beast or be killed; all people will receive a mark in their right hand or in their foreheads; all people must have the mark or the name of the beast, or the number of his name to buy or sell.

The Mark of the Beast

The mark of the beast will undoubtedly be somehow associated with astrology and the worship of the heavens (Ezek. 8:1; 9:1, 4, 6.

"Here is wisdom. Let him that hath understanding count the number of the beast for it is the number of a man; and his number is Six hundred threescore and six" (or 666) (Rev. 13:18).

NOTE:

(1) One must possess wisdom and understanding to "count" the number of the beast. From the earliest of time, the "wise" were the only ones who could calculate the seasons (*"count the number"*) of the heavens to determine time-periods (i.e., the magi or wise men). The wise men *"hath understanding"* of the movements of the heavens.

(2)   The number of the beast is numerical;

(3)   The beast's name is never revealed in Scripture;

(4)   It is the number, or timing, of the beast that will preclude his identity;

(5)   The Six Great Periods of Time (6,000 years) correlate to the Six Ages of the Church (6,000 years).

(6)   The Jewish religious calendar begins in the Spring (the former rain-the First Coming of the Messiah) and the Civil Calendar begins in the Fall (the latter rain-the Second Coming) exactly "SIX" months apart.

(7)   Hebrew is read from right to left;

(8)   The Feast of Trumpets is the First of the Jewish Fall Festivals and the fulfillment of Messianic prophecy;

(9)   Jewish festivals are determined by the Religious Calendar (Ex 12:1-2);

(10)   Spring (Vernal Equinox) changed to Aviv (PE moved from Taurus to Aries;

(11)   Six months later the Civil Calendar begins in the Autumn (Autumnal Equinox, Tishri);

(12)   Six (6) months - Summer Solstice (Leo)

Six (6) months - Vernal Equinox (Taurus)

Six (6) months - Autumnal Equinox (Aquarius)

Six (6) months - Winter Solstice (Scorpius)

(13)   The Six Great Periods of Time reveal the End of the Age and also the identification of the number of the beast "666;"

(14)   The Six periods of Time equal 1/4 of the constellations or three constellations of 2,000 years each **(2,000 x 3 = 6,000 years);**

(15)   The number of the man of the beast is the man of Sagittarius/Scorpius;

(16)   The end of the Ages of "time" occurs when the PE moves to the Vernal Equinox at the mid-point of the constellation of Aquarius and the Winter Solstice at the mid-point of the constellation of Scorpius;

(17) This time-period will most likely occur with the Feast of Trumpets, the Day of Atonement, and lastly the Marriage Supper of the Lamb aligning with the Feast of Tabernacles.

Remember, Daniel 7:10 reads, *"A fiery stream issued and came forth from before him...."* "Fiery stream" in the Talmud, Chagigah 13b, means the Milky Way! Most astronomers will tell you the center of our galaxy is in the direction of the constellation Sagittarius. Then again, in the book of Job 38:31-33 in its reference to the Mazzaroth, *"Canst thou bring forth Mazzaroth in his season?...,"* refers to a "star cluster" within the zodiac and this cluster is the Milky Way. Job 38 is used in the singular form (although implying division of separate chambers) and refers to a man (although it is mostly rendered a plural noun). This description refers to the various planetary deities of the seasons. More importantly the Vulgate translation uses the term for the Milky Way in connotation with Lucifer. ...*"or canst thou guide Arcturus with his sons?"* If you combine all of this with the scripture reference in Revelation 6:2, *"I saw a white horse, and he that sat on him had a bow...and he went forth conquering and to conquer,"* we see the picture of the 666 occurring in the constellations of Sagittarius and Scorpius. John is describing times and persons using the stars and constellations when he refers to the "bow," "crown," the "white horse," "red horse," "black horse," and "pale horse", and the "leopard is synonymous with a Nimrod-type anti-christ."

Now return to the Book of Ezekiel 8:5, *"Then said he unto me, Son of man, lift up thine eyes now the way toward the north. So I lifted up mine eyes the way toward the north, and behold northward at the gate of the altar this image of jealousy in the entry."* Again, the man of Scorpius (aka the likeness of Nimrod, a Babylonian symbol) at the Winter Solstice and the Northern sector of the circle represented in the images of Tammuz and the abominations of the 12 signs of the zodiac.

Those who believe the 12 signs of the zodiac represent the descriptions of the true Messiah may be in for a great awakening and completely taken by surprise because of this great deception. The man of Scorpius, or 666, is also the great deceiver. Thus, in the great constellations of the zodiac we have the confusing depictions of both the Messiah and also the anti-christ.

CHAPTER X

JUDGMENT

The beast will temporarily rule the world for 42 months during the time of the Great Tribulation, *"And all that dwell upon the earth shall worship him, whose names are not written in the book of life..."* (Rev. 13:8); and the Second Beast will perform miracles to deceive the entire world and cause all to worship the First Beast. He will encourage the people of earth to make an image to the First Beast, to receive a mark of identification, and those who would not worship the image would be killed.

In Revelation 14, the Lamb and the 144,000 remnant redeemed from the earth stand ready to do battle. Jesus Christ is still represented as a Lamb here and not yet as the Conqueror.

"And I looked, and, lo, a Lamb stood on the mount Sion, and with him an hundred forty and four thousand, having his Father's name written in their foreheads. And I heard a voice from heaven, as the voice of many waters [many peoples], *and as the voice of a great thunder: and I heard the voice of harpers harping with their harps* [the redeemed of the Lord]. *And they sung as it were a new song before the throne...and no man could learn that song but the hundred and forty and four thousand, which were redeemed from the earth. These are they which were not defiled with women; for*

they are virgins [Spiritually pure and spotless]...*without fault before the throne of God"* (Rev. 14:1-5).

The 144,000 were redeemed as the *"first fruits unto God and the Lamb"* from among men.   They stand without fault before the throne of God in heaven (14:4-5).   The 144,000 represent all who belong to the Lord and those martyred for the Word of their testimony (Rev. 14:13, 15:2).

And then comes judgment and the harvest (Rev. 14:14-20) of the earth:

"And I saw another angel fly in the midst of heaven, having the everlasting gospel to preach unto them that dwell on the earth, and to every nation, and kindred, and tongue, and people. Saying with a loud voice, Fear God, and give glory to him; for the hour of his judgment is come..." (Rev. 14:6-7):

The remainder left on Earth are those warned by the angels preaching the gospel of the impending judgment of God.

"...and worship him that made heaven, and earth, and the sea, and the fountains of waters. And there followed another angel saying, Babylon is fallen, is fallen, that great city, because she made all nations drink of the wine of the wrath of her fornication" (Rev. 14:6-8).

What could possibly be "the wrath of her fornication?" Throughout the Bible, it mentions two types of fornication: (1) sexual immorality; and (2) spiritual fornication—as in Judah, Israel, and an example with Hosea's adulterous wife. It would be hard for a "city" of Babylon to commit a specific immoral sexual act, therefore, it would be best concluded that this description of Babylon in Revelation is indicative of "spiritual" fornication. And this spiritual fornication, among other things, would be perverting the purpose of the heavens and turning them into an idolatrous practice of divination.

Sickles are used to thresh the wheat at harvest time, and this is a depiction of the Second Coming of Jesus Christ. The 7th Trumpet is the Harvest of the earth. *"And another angel came out of the temple..."* (vs. 15).

Interesting that the "temple" is in heaven, *"And another angel came out of the temple which is in heaven..."* (vs. 16). The temple is the New Jerusalem, but it hasn't come down to earth as yet (vs. 17). The harvest must come first; and this is the Harvest of the wicked. *"And another angel came out from the altar, which had power over fire; and cried with a loud cry to him that had the sharp sickle, saying, Thrust in thy sharp sickle, and gather the clusters of the vine of the earth; for her grapes are full ripe" (vs. 15).*

The final Harvest of the Earth occurs at the end of the growing season, just like the farmer's harvest is gathered at the end of the Summer season. *"And the angel thrust in his sickle into the earth, and gathered the vine of the earth, and cast it into the great winepress of the wrath of God..."* (vs. 18-20).

This is the end of the voice of the 7th Angel, and herein is the Sabbath Day Rest depicted throughout the Bible, and only a "rest" for those in Jesus Christ (Rev. 14:13; 15:2-4). Now 7 angels with 7 vials prepare to pour out God's wrath (Rev. 16). Every event in heaven is introduced and followed by a heavenly sign. So, first we know that this will be depicted in heavenly symbols, and these symbols will be portrayed as signs of God's wrath.

Ancient civilizations depicted the heavens as "a great sea" and glass would indicate not only it's clearness but also its transparency. All of those who gained the victory over the beast stood on the sea of glass in heaven. *"And I saw another sign in heaven, great and marvelous, seven angels having the seven last plagues; for in them is filled up the wrath of God..."* (Rev 15:1-2).

. When Jesus ascended into heaven after the resurrection, He disappeared in a cloud, and when Jesus Christ returns again, the Bible describes Him coming in the clouds: ***"And I looked, and behold a white cloud, and upon the cloud one sat like unto the Son of man, having on his head a golden crown, and in his hand a sharp sickle"*** (vs. 14).

It was one of the four beasts who gave the seven angels the golden vials full of the wrath of God. This beast depicts the end of time, as we know it. The fourth beast reveals the time-period at the end and symbolized in the number "7" being the 7,000th year—a time of judgment for the Earth, but a time of rejoicing for the righteous (Rev. 15:2). And this too was a time when no one else could enter through the gates until the plagues of the seven angels were fulfilled.

The First Vial was poured out upon the earth and man. Next comes the judgment of the ELEMENTS OF NATURE [Fire, Air, Earth, and Water] because nature was worshipped as God through astrology/idolatry. Only those with the mark of the beast were affected by the 1st and 5th vials (vs. 16:2): EARTH'S JUDGMENT—man comes from the dust of the Earth; the 2nd vial was poured out upon the sea, the 3rd vial was poured out upon the rivers, and the 6th vial was poured out upon the river Euphrates: WATER'S JUDGMENT.

"And I heard the angel of the waters say, Thou art righteous, O Lord, which art, and was, and shalt be, because thou hast judged thus" (vs. 5).

Judge what? Judgment upon the peoples, nations, and the "seed" of Babylon which spread false doctrines, teachings, idolatry, astrology, and the occult all over the entire face of the Earth.

The 4th judgment falls upon the SUN: THE JUDGMENT OF FIRE; and the 7th vial poured out JUDGMENT upon the AIR.

Rev. 16:13-16 reveal the three unclean spirits associated with the dragon, beast, and false prophet who are gathering together for the battle of Armageddon. Notice "the frogs" which are a symbol of uncleanness come out of their "mouths." These unclean spirits of devils work miracles. They are the anti-christ system which speaks against all that is righteous and reverent toward God.   They represent the Babylonian system judged by God (Rev. 16:19).

"And there came one of the seven angels which had the seven vials, and talked with me, saying unto me, Come hither; I will shew unto thee the judgment of the great whore that sitteth upon many waters.   With whom the kings of the earth have committed fornication, and the inhabitants of the earth have been made drunk with the wine of her fornication.   So he carried me away in the spirit into the wilderness: and I saw a woman sit upon a scarlet coloured beast, full of names of blasphemy, having seven heads and ten horns. And the woman was arrayed in purple and scarlet colour, and decked with gold and precious stones and pearls, having a golden cup in her hand full of abominations and filthiness of her fornication: And upon her forehead was a name written, MYSTERY, BABYLON THE GREAT THE MOTHER OF HARLOTS AND ABOMINATIONS OF THE EARTH. And I saw the woman drunken with the blood of the saints, and with the blood of the martyrs of Jesus: and when I saw her, I wondered with great admiration. And the angel said unto me, Wherefore didst thou marvel? I will tell thee the mystery of the woman, and of the beast that carrieth her, which hath the seven heads and ten horns" (Rev. 17:1-7).

The angel then revealed to John the identity of *"the great whore that sitteth upon many waters."* The waters *"which thou sawest, where the whore sitteth, are peoples, and multitudes, and nations, and tongues"* (vs. 15)—all the peoples of the earth from every nation. And just as the woman of Revelation 12:1 depicts Jerusalem, the woman *"...which thou sawest is that great city, which reigneth over the kings of the earth"* (vs. 18; Rev. 18:1-24) depicts Babylon.

Only those whose names were not written in the book of life (those on earth) "wondered" after the beast (17:8-9).

"And here is the mind which hath wisdom. The seven heads are seven mountains, on which the woman sitteth. And there are seven kings: five are fallen, and one is, and the other is not yet come; and when he cometh, he must continue a short space. And the beast that was, and is not, even he is the eighth, and is of the seven, and goeth into perdition. And the ten horns which thou sawest are ten kings, which have received no kingdom as yet; but receive power as kings one hour with the beast..." (vs. 9-12).

Again, the angel reveals to John that the ten kings *"hate the whore, and shall make her desolate"* (vs. 16). Then comes the depiction of the destruction of Babylon (Rev. 18:1-24).

"And after these things I heard a great voice of much people in heaven, saying, Al-le-lu'-ia, Salvation, and glory, and honour, and power, unto the Lord our God" (Rev. 19:1).

Notice these were people in heaven who praised God for judging the "great whore." Now time is closing, and the 24 elders and the 4 beasts fall down and worship God (vs. 4). Interesting to note that up until this point many people were in heaven, but the Marriage Supper of the Lamb has not occurred until Revelation 19:1

In Revelation 19:11, heaven opens and the white horse with its Rider comes forth to make war with the armies of heaven (19:14). This is a depiction of Jesus Christ (vs. 11) standing poised with the remnant seed of Revelation 14 and the army of heaven (Rev. 19:14). And just as He is depicted in the beginning chapters of the Book of Revelation (7-20) as the Alpha, He is also portrayed toward the ending chapters of Revelation as the Omega. John reveals Jesus Christ in the beginning of Revelation (1:14) and near the end of Revelation (19:12). Here again, two riders on two white horses have been revealed in Revelation—Chapter 6:2 and 19:11. The symbol of destruction in Chapter 6 (the anti-christ) and the symbol of righteousness in Chapter 19:11—Jesus Christ.

The beast with his armies have been gathering (Ch. 16:13-16) to make war against the KING OF KINGS, AND LORD OF LORDS—no longer pictured as a Lamb but as a Conquering King. Revelation 19:20 reveals the victory goes to Christ, and the beast and false prophet were cast *"alive into a lake of fire burning with brimstone."* Satan is bound for 1,000 years, known as the Millennium, until he is released for "a little season."

During the time satan is bound for 1,000 years, believers live and reign with Jesus Christ, and *"And I saw thrones, and they sat upon them: and I saw the souls* [Greek word 'psuche,' meaning spirits] *of them that were beheaded for the witness of Jesus and for the word of God...this is the first resurrection"* (vs. 4-5); but the rest of the dead who followed the beast *"...lived not again until the thousand years were finished..."* (vs. 5). For those in the first resurrection came rejoicing and eternal rest; for those who died without Christ comes the second death and judgment after the 1,000 years of the Millennium.

After the 1,000 years, Satan will again be released and go to the nations to deceive them and where he will gather all people from the four corners of the earth [the number of whom is as the sand of the sea], to the battle of Gog and Magog.

"And they went up on the breadth of the earth, and compassed the camp of the saints about, and the beloved city..." [Jerusalem] (vs. 8); *"and fire came down from God out of heaven, and devoured them. And the devil that deceived them was cast into the lake of fire and brimstone, where the beast and the false prophet are, and shall be tormented day and night for ever and ever"* (vs.10). *And I saw a great white*

throne, and him that sat on it, from whose face the earth and the heaven fled away... " (vs. 11). This is the end of time. The heavens revealed the season, the time, etc., but *"...there was found no place for them."*

The Great White Throne Judgment

"And I saw a great white throne...And I saw the dead, small and great, stand before God; and the books were opened: and another book was opened, which is the book of life: and the dead were judged out of those things which were written in the books, according to their works. And the sea gave up the dead which were in it; and death and hell delivered up the dead which were in them: and they were judged every man according to their works. And death and hell were cast into the lake of fire. This is the second death. And whosoever was not found written in the book of life was cast into the lake of fire" (vs. 11-15).

The Great White Throne judgment is reserved only for the second death. The books are opened and the dead stand before God to be judged, *"...and the dead were judged out of those things which were written in the books, according to their works...And death and hell were cast into the lake of fire. This is the second death. And whosoever was not found written in the book of life was cast into the lake of fire (Rev. 20:11-15).*

A New Heaven and A New Earth

Revelation 21:1 and Isaiah 65:17-18 speak of the same: *"...for, behold, I create Jerusalem a rejoicing, and her people a joy." "...Behold, I make all things new..."* (Rev. 21:5). *"And I saw a new heaven and a new earth; for the first heaven, and the first earth were passed away; and there was no more sea. And I John saw the holy city, new Jerusalem, coming down from God out of heaven, prepared as a bride adorned for her husband"* (vs. 1).

This picture depicts the Jewish wedding festival. Who is the bride, the Lamb's wife? It is *"...that great city, the holy Jerusalem, descending out of heaven from God"* (vs. 10). The closing chapters of the Book of Revelation bring to believers the fulfillment of the Feast of Tabernacles where God dwells with His people (Rev. 7:15; 21:3).

For seven days the bride and groom are secluded in the "chupah" and after the consummation of their marriage, they exit where the wedding feast occurs in another week-long celebration (see John 3:29). And this is the Marriage Supper of the Lamb (the Feast of Tabernacles), *"And I heard a great voice out of heaven saying, Behold, the tabernacle of God is with men, and he will dwell with them, and they shall be his people, and God himself shall be with them, and be their God"* (vs. 3). *"For, behold, I create new heavens and a new earth: and the former shall not be remembered nor come into mind"* (Isaiah 65:17).

Now it is finished...there is no time because there is no heaven, as we know it, *"...And the city had no need of the sun, neither the moon, to shine in it: for the glory of God did lighten it, and the Lamb is the light thereof"* (vs. 23); and a different earth as we know it, *"..for the first earth were passed away; and there was no more sea"* (vs 1).

Then John is given the measurements of the New Jerusalem, with 12 gates with the names of the 12 tribes of the children of Israel (vs. 12). The city was foursquare shaped with equal length and heighth. The gates consisted of 3 gates on the East, 3 gates on the North, 3 gates on the South, and 3 gates on the West. Twelve foundations made up the walls of the golden city consisting of precious stones with the names of the 12 Apostles written in them.

The city "lieth foursquare" and measured 12,000 furlongs (12,000 x 2 = 24,000 priests, Levites, remnant, Saints x 6 Ages = 144,000) (Rev. 21:16). The symbolic 144,000 represents the entire "remnant" of God who dwell in the New Jerusalem. This is made known to us through the measure of the wall which measured 144 cubits (1 cubit = 1,000 x 144 = 144,000). The measure of a man is "6" (1 cubit = 1,000 x 6 = 6,000).   Six thousand (6,000) years is the measurement of mankind's allotted Time. Here too, is found the measurement of Time represented by the 24 Elders of Revelation (144,000 divided by 6,000 years = 24); and the 4 Beasts of Revelation (24 Elders divided by 4 Beasts = 6 Ages) reveal the 6 Ages or 6,000 years of Time.—This measures the completion of the Mystery of God.

"And I saw no temple therein: for the Lord God Almighty and the Lamb are the temple of it" (21:22). In the midst of the New Jerusalem, out of the throne of God, flows the crystal clear "water of life" and on either side of it "the tree of life" producing 12 manner of fruits each month. *"And there shall be no more curse: but the throne of God and of the Lamb shall be in it, and his servants shall serve him: And they shall see his face, and his name shall be in their foreheads. And there shall be no night there; and they need no candle, neither light of the sun; for the Lord God giveth them light; and they shall reign for ever and ever..."* (22:3-7). And the Lord said,

"...Behold, I come quickly..."

According to the 7,000 year time-line of Abraham, the world will go through a violent upheavel...the earth clock rests precariously at the 12th hour nearing the end of the 6,000th year...

...are you ready?

...an appointed hour
...an appointed day
...an appointed month
...an appointed year

...AN APPOINTED SEASON

Where do you think the catching away (rapture) of the Church will occur —pre, mid, or post tribulation?

THE LAMB

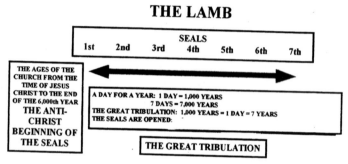

			SEALS			
1st	2nd	3rd	4th	5th	6th	7th

THE AGES OF THE CHURCH FROM THE TIME OF JESUS CHRIST TO THE END OF THE 6,000th YEAR **THE ANTI-CHRIST BEGINNING OF THE SEALS**

A DAY FOR A YEAR: 1 DAY = 1,000 YEARS
7 DAYS = 7,000 YEARS
THE GREAT TRIBULATION: 1,000 YEARS = 1 DAY = 7 YEARS
THE SEALS ARE OPENED:

THE GREAT TRIBULATION

ANGELS

JUDGMENTS

SEVEN TRUMPETS

GOD'S

WRATH

SEVEN VIALS

THE MARRIAGE SUPPER OF THE LAMB

THE NEW JERUSALEM

REFERENCES

1. Wiseman (trans), *Tertullian*, 1849.
2. Whiston, *Josephus, Antiquities*, Book III, Ch. VI
3. Whiston, *Josephus on Philo*
4. *Ibid., Ant. I, I3*
5. Augustine, *Commentaries on the Psalms*, Ch. II.
6. Drummond, Sir Wm., *Essay on the Science of the Egyptians and Chaldeans*, 1824.
7. Whiston, *Josephus, Antiquities*, Book I, Chap. VII, Pg. 49
8. Maclear, G.F., *Lightfoot's Commentary on the Galatians*, New Testament History, London, 1866, Pg. 363
9. Hurst, George Leopold, B.D., *An Outline of the History of Christian Literature*, Macmillan Co., NY, 1926.
10. Sanders, Frank Knight, Ph.D., *History of the Hebrews*, Charles Scribner's Sons, NY, 1905, Pg. 110.
11. Rolleston, F., *Mazzaroth*, 1862, Pg. 51.
12. Ibid, Ibn Ezra, 1812.
13. Wiseman (trans), Lib 5, advers Haeres, 1849.
14. Midrash Tanhuma, Kedoshim 10.
15. Shirley Ann Miller, "The Magi: In Search of Messiah," 1999, pg. 93):
16. Shirley Ann Miller, Selected notes from a published manuscript, "Astrology: Myths and Legends," 1982.
17. Shirley Ann Miller, "The Covenant: A Promise Written in the Stars," 1997

GENERAL BIBLIOGRAPHY

Albright,W.F.,"The Biblical Period," Biblical Colloq,1950.

Aratus,Solensis,"Aratus(WithCallimachus and Lycophron) (Loeb Edition; N.Y: G.P. Putnam's Sons, 1921.

Bartholomaeo, S., "Systema Bralimanicum," Rome, 1802, trans. Wiseman, 1835.

Burnett, John, Early Greek Philosophy (Second Edition; N.Y.: The Macmillan Co., 1909).

Coleman, Christopher B., Constantine the Great and Christianity, NY, Columbia U. Press, 1914.

Cumont, Franz, "Astrology and Religion Among the Greeks and Romans, New York, Putnam, 1912.

Dean, James Elmer (Trans.), "Epiphanius, Treatise on Weights and Measures, Chicago, The University of Chicago Press, 1935.

Delambre, "History of Ancient Astronomy," 1775.

Delambre, "Astronomy of the Middle Ages," 1819, trans. Wiseman, 1835.

Dowling, John, The History of Romanism, From the Earliest Corruptions of Christianity, NY, 1871

Farrar, F.W., The Early Days of Christianity, NY, 1882.

Humboldt, A. von, "Cosmos: A Sketch of the Physical Desc. of the Universe," Bell and Daldy, London, 1871.

Jackson, A.V.W., "Zoroaster, the Prophet of Ancient Iran," New York, 1899.

Josephus, Jewish Wars, Book II.

Kent, R.G., "The Recently Published Old Persian Inscriptions," Journal of the American Oriental Society, LI, 1991.

Rainy, Robert, D.D., The Ancient Catholic Church, Charles Scribner's Sons, NY, 1902.

Spalding, M.J., Evidences of Catholicity, John Murphy, MD, 1865.